So Ask

POETS ON POETRY

David Lehman, General Editor
Donald Hall, Founding Editor

Philip Levine

So Ask

ESSAYS, CONVERSATIONS, AND INTERVIEWS

Ann Arbor

THE UNIVERSITY OF MICHIGAN PRESS

2005   2004   2003   2002   4   3   2   1

A CIP catalog record for this book is available from the British Library.

Library of Congress Cataloging-in-Publication Data

Levine, Philip, 1928–
    So ask : essays, conversations, and interviews / Philip Levine.
      p. cm. — (Poets on poetry)
    ISBN 0-472-09420-3 (cloth : alk. paper) —
    ISBN 0-472-06420-7 (pbk. : alk. paper)
    1. Levine, Philip, 1928—Interviews.   2. Poets, American—
20th century—Interviews.   3. Poetry—Authorship.
4. Poetics.   I. Title.   II. Series.

PS3562.E9 Z475   2002
811'.54—dc21
[B]   2002020293

ACKNOWLEDGMENTS
Thanks to these publications for permission to reprint the following
material:
American Poet, "Interview with Edward Hirsch," 1999; "Larry Levis,"
1996. *Atlantic Unbound,* "Interview with Wen Stephenson," 1999.
DoubleTake, "On First Looking into John Keats' Letters," 1998.
Image, "Interview with Paul Mariani," 1996. *Manoa,* "Neruda y Yo,"
1991. *Michigan Quarterly Review,* "Two Journeys," 1997. *Missouri
Review,* "Craft Non-Lecture," 1987. *The Threepenny Review,* "Beauty
and/or Truth," 1994. *Tri-Quarterly,* "Conversation with Harry
Thomas's English Class, Davidson College," 1995. *Vanderbilt Review,*
"Conversation with Poet Kate Daniels," 1995.

For Paul Mariani

Preface

Twenty years ago I assembled a collection of eight interviews, which was published by the University of Michigan Press under the title *Don't Ask*. I was forty-four years old when the earliest interview was conducted, fifty-one at the time of the last. In other words I was middle-aged and in mid-career, my poetry was beginning to receive widespread attention and gain notices, not all of them good, but I was optimistic about what lay ahead. I'm pleased to be able to say I've kept on writing, the work has continued to receive attention, not all of it good, and I look forward to more years as a writer.

Rereading the preface to *Don't Ask*, I found a younger, more energetic, sprightlier, and sassier me. I also found a man of greater political commitment and hope than the one writing these words, a man who still believed in the possibility of an America for all of us, one who at times felt compelled to make much of his radical loyalties and to advertise his belief in the anarchism of the early Christians, of William Blake, and especially of the Spaniards who in order to build a truly humane society struggled against the tyranny of church, army, and state until their movement was crushed by Franco's repressive forces. As often as possible—in both prose and verse—I referred to Buenaventura Durruti's visionary announcement that we carried a new world here in our hearts, a world that was growing minute by minute. I believed it, and then I did not. I think there was no crucial event. I let myself be ground down by the passage of time, by the steady flow of defeats, by the knowledge that the country had grown far more materialistic and cynical. Alas, my character was not up to my ideals.

The earliest interviews and conversations collected in the present volume were conducted after I turned sixty-four, and they reflect a very different person, one who had entered a stage of life for which we aging Americans seem to have no word or phrase, though when my grandfather was this age I had no doubt he was "old," ditto for my mother. I doubt I'm any wiser than when I completed the earlier collection, though I may appear so, for I am both less energetic and less angry. I believe my sense of humor is still intact though less zany. My hope is that my more "measured" stance is not an effort to sound wise. This is not a book of wisdom.

What sort of book is it then? It's largely a series of efforts to respond to certain questions, some concerned with my personal experiences, some dealing with my life as a writer, others dealing with larger themes such as the relationship between poetry and politics or between decency and beauty. Many of these questions were first posed to me and others by other poets, journalists, poetry lovers, and students of poetry. My hope is that these interviews, conversations, and essays will be of some use to those who read poetry—especially the poetry of the recent past—for the energy, vision, and truths it often contains. There are also the personal tributes to people who have been especially valuable to me both as a man and a writer and to writers who had a special significance for me when I began taking poetry seriously.

A good deal has happened to American poetry since those earlier interviews; some of it I view positively, such as the ever-growing popularity of poetry in this country and the extraordinary variety of the poetry itself, but once again our poets seem divided into small, mutually exclusive camps, which to me is not a cause for celebration. Some of the worst aspects of today's poetry scene have been with us since my first entrance into this arena and probably much longer: the prestige of murky, pretentious writing and the abhorrence of any poetry concerned with such practical matters as hunger, shelter, and survival, much less equality and exploitation. We still have "revolutionary" and "reactionary" movements that claim to be marginalized even while they dominate the university writing departments and many of the classiest magazines and presses. As Grace Paley once remarked, "Everything changes except the *avant-garde.*" Many of the concerns of this collection are much the same as those of *Don't Ask*, but the voice and vision are a little less combative and hopeful.

Only a few of these interviews are printed here exactly as they were in their original journal incarnations. Upon rereading them I discovered I had a talent for steering the conversation to a few set subjects and then making statements I felt loyal to or comfortable with. Either that or—less likely—my interviewers were obsessed with the same questions. In any event, once I found myself reading the same scenarios over and over I tried to remove the redundancies so that the book itself could be more varied. None of these essays was written after 9/11, so you won't find any of the glossy and self-indulgent "Patriotism" that has sickened our culture or even a half-assed effort to combat it. (There is a lot of work waiting for the poets of America.) Nor will you find the self-censorship so many feared would be the result of our present wars, the domestic and the other one. American poetry will not be silenced; it will carry on the search for its own soul, that soul—as Whitman wrote—that possesses a "measureless pride which revolts from any lesson but its own."

Contents

I. Essays

On First Looking into
John Keats's Letters

I found the work of John Keats in my twenty-first year, and it has guided and inspired me ever since. I count as the work not only the poems and the amazing letters but the life as well, which I encountered in the biographies of Sidney Colvin and Amy Lowell and later in those of Aileen Ward, Robert Gittings, and Walter Jackson Bate. I also found suggestions of the work of the living man in hundreds of relevant pages of the writings of those who made up "The Keats Circle," pages I pored over in the stacks of the Wayne University library in Detroit in my hunger to devour this early hero.

My formal education, such as it was, was bequeathed to me by the Detroit public schools, and I believed then and still believe they did well by me. Math, history, French, chemistry, physics, English composition, literature, and physical education were all taught with rigor and skill. It was not, however, until my junior year in high school that I encountered a poem that seemed relevant to the life I'd experienced or the one I believed was waiting for me. My literature teacher, Mrs. Paperno, a small, dark-haired, intense woman, read to the class one day a short poem by Wilfred Owen. "Did you all hear that?" she asked in her most severe voice, and even the football players in the class nodded their assent, for Mrs. Paperno commanded respect from all of us. The poem was "Arms and the Boy":

From *Doubletake*, "On First Looking into John Keats's Letters," 1998.

Let the boy try along this bayonet blade
How cold steel is, and keen with hunger of blood;
Blue with all malice, like a madman's flash;
And thinly drawn with famishing for flesh.

Lend him to stroke these blind, blunt bullet-leads,
Which long to nuzzle in the hearts of lads,
Or give him cartridges whose fine zinc teeth
Are sharp with the sharpness of grief and death.

For his teeth seem for laughing round an apple.
There lurk no claws behind his fingers supple;
And God will grow no talons at his heels,
Nor antlers through the thickness of his curls.

How Mrs. Paperno divined the power this poem had over me I do not know, but as the class broke up at the end of the hour she offered to loan me the little collection of Owens's poetry if I promised to bring it back on Monday. I promised, and the book was mine for an entire weekend. World War II was still raging in Europe and the Pacific, and seventeen-year-olds expected to complete high school and enter the military. What we were supposed to feel about this I gathered from the talk of my elders, my classmates, and the movies I saw was some sort of profound inner swelling of the organs of patriotism. Of course, that was not what I felt at all; I was simply horrified at the thought of being maimed or killed or being forced to maim and kill others. In poem after poem Owen authenticated my own response to the carnage I might have to participate in. He had been there, he had seen it and finally died from it. His poems, which seethed with his disgust for the "Great War," as it was then known, went a long way toward assuring me that my response to the thought of battle was not insane.

Like many young people, I had been writing something I hesitated then and would hesitate now to call poetry, though what else it might have been I don't know. Perhaps I should just call it bad poetry. These compositions were relatively short—I could recite any one in less than ten minutes (they were never written down)—they were unrhymed, and not in any fixed metrical pattern. Their rhetorical structures were based largely on the more adventurous sermons I heard on the radio on Sunday mornings. Their most common subjects were simple and present: rain, wind, earth (dirt, that is), snow, the night sky, the thickly clustered trees in the undeveloped, wooded blocks near our house, and the birds that thrived there. No doubt part of the intensity of pleasure I derived from composing these first poems during my nightly sojourns came from the fact that I avoided what bothered me most in my daily life: family life, anti-Semitism (which flourished in the Detroit of that—Father Coughlin's—era), sex, and the waiting war. I leaped immediately to a "higher" level and was conscious even then that every poem flung out at the night sky was an effort to use, perhaps luxuriate in, my separateness and possibly to bridge the great moat between me and all other living creatures. Of course, like many beginning poets my age then and perhaps now, I avoided the beneficial influence of the poetry of others, at least until my encounter with the work of Wilfred Owen, but even his stylistic influence on me was minimal, for I found his rhythmic structures and his experiments with rhyme daunting. What I grasped for and fumbled with was his richly textured phrasing. His "The shrill, demented choirs of wailing shells" became something like my "The night wind's wail dies daily into prayer." Bad as these early efforts were, at least now they had the model of true poetry.

Then quite suddenly the following summer the war ended, and I was allowed to consider alternatives to the military. I enrolled in Wayne, the city university of Detroit, and it was there I quickly encountered the poets who would have the most significant influence on my writing and thinking. For almost two weeks Stephen Crane became my model:

I Saw a Man Pursuing the Horizon

I saw a man pursuing the horizon;
Round and round they sped.
I was disturbed at this;
I accosted the man.
"It is futile," I said.
"You can never—"

> "You lie," he cried,
> And ran on.

It took me a day to do a passable imitation of that and the other little gnomic poems and ten more days to tire of them; it was just too easy. Then T. S. Eliot became my lord and master until in my second semester I encountered his jew (with a small *j*) in the poem "Gerontion," squatting on a window sill, "spawned," if you will, in some Belgian whorehouse. Then it was the leftist, pre-Munich poetry of Auden and Spender, and later Hart Crane, whose impenetrability convinced me not only of his greatness but the wisdom of my own aesthetic, which might have been described as "make it obscure," which comes quite naturally when so little of your world is clear to you.

Then came one of the crucial decisions of my life in poetry: the choice between Dr. Gene Sax and Professor A. D. Wooly, that is the choice between the fashionable poets of that hour— Hopkins, Yeats, Eliot, Pound, and Stevens—taught brilliantly by Dr. Sax, the most elegant and seductive tenured member of the English Department, and the all but forgotten stars of a previous era, the Romantic poets, taught with fading fervor by old Professor Wooly, whose life work in scholarship was a small portion of the editing of the complete letters of Horace Walpole.

Tall, lean, costumed like a banker, Dr. Sax taught with a subdued theatricality. He used no notes but employed the blackboard ceaselessly as he paced back and forth before the front of the class, stopping every few moments to add lines or arrows to his diagram of the day's poem, or if the poem were as dense as Yeats's "Byzantium" an entire class period could be consumed with the explication of a single passage. (In 1947 the New Criticism was not all that new, but it had only recently made its way to Detroit.) I sat watching my classmates scribbling into their textbooks as the poem itself disappeared beneath a maze of notes and connecting vertical and horizontal lines. I think we all went away from these breathtaking performances convinced that a poem worthy of the name was at least as inscrutable as the Rosetta stone. What would we find in our anthologies when we got home? Certainly not the poem, for that had been replaced by a complex and brilliant tapestry woven by Dr. Sax. I never figured out why Sax could draw fifty to seventy-five students, including a scattering of the most elegant and depressed women on campus, long-haired lionesses who sat glumly in their tailored suits seemingly mesmerized by Sax's articularity. The assignments were small, rarely as many as a half-dozen poems, and Dr. Sax was far too occupied with his explications to find out if any of the poems had been read by the students.

Professor Wooley, on the other hand, thought nothing of assigning sixty pages of poetry for a single meeting. The class was expected to digest all of *The Lyrical Ballads* between Monday and Wednesday and to pay special attention to the famous preface. Whereas Sax chain-smoked Camels as he paced the classroom, Wooly sat, head down, drawing on an unlighted pipe and read aloud key passages from the assigned pages. His commentaries scarcely needed to be noted; they went something like, "This goes to the heart of the matter" or "Here is the poet at the height of his powers." He once stated that Coleridge never wrote a bad line and then seemed so stunned by the boldness of his assertion that he sat in silence for a long minute before the dozen of us who had survived the three-week rampage through Wordsworth. A large rumpled man with a great head of gray hair going white, he would sit silently at his desk when the hour ended, as though lost in thought or exhausted by our presence as we took leave of the room in silence.

Even now it seems unlikely that I would have dropped Dr. Sax's class and stuck with Professor Wooly's. As unsophisticated as I was in my second year of college, I knew this was not superior classroom teaching, for I had encountered that in high school. It may have had something to do with Wooly's patience; he seemed willing to wait for as long as it took for us to realize the majesty and power of the poetry he was bustling us through. Perhaps I felt I couldn't desert the other eleven students or perhaps it was Professor Wooly I could not desert, for there was something genuine and dear about his befuddled manner. I'm sure I appreciated the lack of a performance, for already I had discovered how common performers were in the university. I sensed an unstated faith on Wooly's part that if we welcomed these poems into our hearts and minds they would achieve themselves without an insistence on his part. The case was sealed when, after a quiet reading of "Frost at Midnight," Wooly looked up at the class and said, "There is something here for each of us." I believe it was in the "for each of us," the acknowledgment that in the face of Coleridge's genius we were all merely humble workers in the fields of poetry.

After a sideways glance at Southey lasting only a single meeting, we raced first through Byron and then Shelley and with four weeks left in the semester arrived at young John Keats and his first tentative efforts at poetry, the imitations of Spenser. It suddenly appeared as though Professor Wooly had tired of his own method; perhaps he had a special fondness for Keats, or as an experienced teacher he may have been responding to the unstated urgings of the class. At any rate the pace of our reading slowed drastically. It is possible he recognized the special place Keats could occupy in the spiritual lives we were in the process of creating. We were twelve young and not so young men and women from the city of Detroit, from working-class or lower-middle-class backgrounds. The class met in the late afternoon, and some members hurried to it after finishing the day shift at one of the local factories. Even our costumes revealed that. With Keats there was an immediate affinity we had not felt before. Wordsworth and Coleridge seemed to have stepped as poets directly into their maturity—in Wordsworth's case even middle age—at the beginning of their careers. Shelley and Byron were nothing if not exotic aristocrats, and they rode far above us, above even the clouds of industrial garbage that hovered over our university. In important ways Keats was one of us: young, uncertain, determined, decently educated at mediocre schools, and struggling both to survive and to believe in the necessity of his art. He was what one of us might have been had one of us been phenomenal John Keats.

From the moment I first read "On First Looking into Chapman's Homer" I was hooked. The poem expressed perfectly my own response to the great Romantic poetry I was reading for the first time and—to use Keats's expression—feeling on my pulse as I had felt no poetry before.

> Much I have travell'd in the realms of gold,
>   And many goodly states and kingdoms seen;
>   Round many western islands have I been
> Which bards in fealty to Apollo hold.
> Oft of one wide expanse had I been told
>   That deep-brow'd Homer ruled as his demesne;
>   Yet did I never breathe its pure serene
> Till I heard Chapman speak out loud and bold:
> Then felt I like some watcher of the skies
>   When a new planet swims into his ken;
> Or like stout Cortez when with eagle eyes
>   He star'd at the Pacific—and all his men
> Look'd at each other with a wild surmise—
>   Silent, upon a peak in Darien.

I was dazzled by the fullness of expression, the daring of the figures, the sheer audacity of the conception, and the sonnet form fulfilled to perfection. The truth was, half of me never believed it at all: I was a skeptical big-city boy. But another part of me cared not at all about belief, for the language itself was so delicious I read and reread the poem until without trying I'd memorized it. How could poetry be better than this? I asked myself, and as I read deeper into his work the answer came to me.

I do not know if Professor Wooly knew that my ambition was to become a poet; I'd shared this hope with very few people. Detroit was not Greenwich Village, Cambridge, or even Berkeley; it taught you not to advertise all of your ambitions. Its stance was ferociously masculine, and most of its citizens seemed to have little interest in or tolerance for the arts or for what might be described as "artistic behavior." Even half the women I went to Wayne with carried themselves as though they yearned to become professional bowlers. My guess is that Wooly, like Mrs. Paperno before him, divined certain needs in me and did his best to meet them, for like her he proved to have an extraordinarily generous nature.

It must have been concern for my spiritual nature that

prompted Professor Wooly one late afternoon as the last of daylight faded across his desk to hand me a volume of the letters of Keats opened to the page concerned with what the poet called "The vale of Soul-making." Keats distinguishes between the "sparks of divinity in millions" that are not yet souls and the souls they become when they "acquire identities" and "each one is personally itself." He goes on to ask how the sparks become individual identities and answers with a question: "How, but by the medium of a world like this?" While I read on in a state bordering on amazement, the professor cut an apple into eight nearly equal segments, which he laid out on his desk between us. In what I read, a man barely older than I was attempting to account for the function of human pain and suffering in the creation of the human spirit. For a brief moment I had a vision of the whole person I might become in "a world like ours," and in that moment I found, to use his words, "the use of the world" for probably the first time in my life. "I will call the *world* a School," Keats had written, "instituted for the purpose of teaching little children to read—I will call the *Human heart* the *horn Book* used in that School—and I will call *the Child able to read, the Soul* made from that *School* and its *hornbook*. Do you not see how necessary a World of Pains and troubles is to school an Intelligence and make it a Soul?" For a moment I saw. Nothing I had read before had so potently lifted the gloom that hovered over my small portion of Detroit. In my excitement I reached for a slice of Wooly's apple and popped it into my mouth. A silence. Wooly sighed almost imperceptibly and, being the gentleman he was, offered me a second perfect eighth, which I had the good sense to decline. Again like Mrs. Paperno before him, Professor Wooly loaned me the volume for the weekend. I remember with what care I held the book under my arm on the long bus ride back to my apartment and how I hoped that in the days to follow some of its wisdom might pass into me. Perhaps it did.

This was 1948, some ten years before Americans of my generation would set about the creation of a body of poetry that would later be labeled as "confessional" and even longer before those poets' acts of self destruction, but the models were already there. Had not the most gifted boy wonder of the American century, Hart Crane, shown us all that the true poet was the poet *manque?* That year Detroit itself would welcome Dylan Thomas, then the most dazzling wordsmith in the English-speaking world, but it was not the gaunt, tousled bard of the photographs who mesmerized us with his voice but a bloated, stained, lurching, tiny version of W. C. Fields to whom the tall and elegant women flocked. My mentor to be, John Berryman, would later claim that what the poet required above all else was a wounding so terrible that he or she could only barely survive it. The accepted belief was that the poet wrote out of the source of his agony until he or she could no longer, and then came the leap from the stern of a ship bound to NYC or from a bridge spanning the Mississippi. Imagine my relief and surprise when Professor Wooly handed me a volume of the letters opened to the following passage: "Whenever I find myself growing vaporish I rouse myself, wash, and put on a clean shirt, brush my hair and clothes, tie my shoestrings neatly, and in fact adonize as I were going out—then all clean and comfortable I sit down to write. This I find the greatest relief." A poet writing out of his joy in the world and in himself, out of what Coleridge had called his "genial spirits." What a relief for me after all the talk of creative mutilation. It seemed quite suddenly I could be both a poet and a person, dare I say a mensch, even in a world like ours, that is if I were able to create such a person out of what I'd been given.

What did I make of Keats's famous Negative Capability letter? When only twenty-two years old he had written his two brothers that in a "disquisition" with a friend "several things dove-tailed in my mind, and at once it struck me what quality went to form a Man of Achievement, especially in Literature, and which Shakespeare possessed so enormously—I mean Negative Capability, that is, when a man is capable of being in uncertainties, mysteries, doubts, without any irritable reaching after fact and reason—." If I understood him fully I did not take him to mean I could stop thinking and live the rest of my life as a cabbage or even take too seriously the thrush who in Keats's own sonnet advises the young poet not to fret after knowledge. Wooly, good academic that he was, had already drawn my attention to the letter in which the poet stated he meant to follow Solomon's direction and "get wisdom—get understanding." Keats had written that there was but one way for him: "the road lies through application, study, and thought." By this time, even at age twenty, certain things were clear to me. One was that Keats was a genius and I was not, and so I would have to apply myself with even greater dedication than he if I were to write anything worthy of a human life. Another was that his early poems—like the early poems of Hart Crane, which I already knew—gave not the least hint of what was to come. Great poet that he was, Keats did not spring fully formed from the mind of God. Though not as hopeless as mine, his first efforts were poor, and what finally mattered was that he had done just what he had set out to do—he had made himself a poet and he had done this while living "in uncertainties, mysteries, doubts, without any irritable reaching after fact and reason." In other words, according to Keats, if my intention were to become a poet, my ability to write in a world I did not understand and from which I did not demand final answers might prove to be an asset rather than a defect of character. At that time I lived among men and women my own age or slightly older who often took my refusal to search after "fact and reason" as a sign of sloth or indifference. I had known it was part of who I was but had not assigned it a label. My friends would become the mathematicians, historians, philosophers, and linguists of my generation. Gifted with Negative Capability and Keats's map of the road toward poetry, I might set out with realistic hopes. Unlike Lord Byron or Shelley, I was not the scion of a great family. Like Keats, I was descended from ordinary people, in my case ordinary people with extraordinary minds and imaginations. This lack of class or family with a capital *F* could, I realized even then, prove to be a virtue, for it meant that, like Keats, I could not live apart from the daily difficulties of the world. I had somehow to support myself and those I might become responsible for. I could regard these circumstances as a terrible distraction, the Alps that stood between me and the poetry I might write, or like Keats I could regard them as an opportunity to become an adult; I could regard them as part of the material out of which I might build my character and later my poetry. I chose to try to follow the model I found in his letters and in his life. Unlike Keats, I was gifted with good health; I lived long enough to bless the needs that placed me in the company of the men and women who became my poetry.

For the final meeting of Professor Wooly's class there was no reading assignment, and when the dozen of us assembled we had no idea what to expect. Somewhat shyly he thanked us for our attention and our good work. "I know this poetry has gone out of fashion, which should tell you the value of fashion," he said, "for there is no poetry more necessary for the growth of our spirits." He announced that he had saved this period to read a few things to us, though he assured us that he knew he was not a gifted reader of poetry. Nonetheless, he read the "Ode to Psyche" and the great late ode "To Autumn" with remarkable authority, for in truth he had a deep, resonant voice, and when he slowed the pace of his reading he could be an impressive reader. He then opened a volume of the Buxton Forman edition of the letters and read to us from the October 1818 letter to Woodhouse in which the poet discusses the lack of identity of the poet. "What shocks the virtuous philosopher delights the camelion poet," and he looked up at us with a delighted smile and went on. "The poet is the most unpoetical of any thing in existence, because he has no identity," and finished with Keats's assurance to Woodhouse that he meant to do the world some good, though that might have to wait for his maturer years, for first he had to reach "as high a summit in Poetry as the nerve bestowed upon" him would suffer. Professor Wooly closed the book. "Keats has told us," he said, "that he has no sense of his own identity; he is constantly filling some other body possessing an unchangeable attribute, some creature of impulse, and yet each of us in this room has an overwhelming sense of the identity of John Keats, who has entered our lives through his writing for as long as we live." He bowed his head for a moment. "Isn't that remarkable! He requires us, his readers."

Though the semester ended, my reading of Keats did not. I was deep into the Colvin biography, and I read on to the end watching those terrible months unfold. I can still recall completing the book in a brightly lit annex of the Wayne library and feeling as though something enormous had been stolen from me, from all of us who love poetry, and feeling also the terrible injustice of a world that produces a poetic genius of this quality once a century and then takes the life before that talent is fulfilled. I thought then as I've thought so many times since of the poems that might have been ours and the enormous literary reputation that might have been his had he lived his three score and ten. It is curious and wonderful to realize that the man who has served as my mentor and model all these years was one third my present age when he passed from poetry. Wonderful too, it seems to me, that I found him at Wayne, a campus of seedy old homes and temporary buildings bursting with the new students the postwar years deposited. Rereading his poems, his letters, his life now, I'm not sure what I regret the most. I think it was the denial of his simple daily life, for who else have I encountered through life or books who lived that life with such intensity and fullness? I think too of the loss of daily human contact with all those he would have encountered. Hard to imagine the power and grace his presence would have conferred on those he would have touched. At times I hear it as an unseen wave of genial caring breaking forever on the farthest human shore. But what he left us and what we will celebrate as long as our language survives is unique, for even though he lived to be only twenty-five he is with all of us, an extraordinary human soul animating us still.

Beauty and/or Truth

The second time I became a poet was in the autumn of 1947; I was nineteen, a sophomore at Wayne University in Detroit whose intention it was to obtain a degree in engineering. Unfortunately or fortunately, depending on how you look at it, one Saturday I fell off a ladder while attempting to place a storm window on one of my mother's upstairs bedroom windows. I not only shattered the glass, I also broke my right wrist on the porch railing that came up to meet me. The following Monday my instructor in mechanical drawing informed me that it was too late to drop the course and not receive a failing grade. I could attend class or not attend; in any case, unless I completed all the assignments I would flunk. I decided late that afternoon that if this man was representative of the world of engineers I might better spend my time with other people.

Like many young Americans, I had begun writing poetry long before I read any poetry that excited me. That was the first time I became a poet, at age fourteen, a career I pursued in secret for close to two years and then for no reason I can recall abandoned. None of the poems of that era survives, for none was put to paper. I have a strong sense of what they sounded like and what their subjects were, but I will spare you. I still harbor a small faith that the poetry of many other fourteen-year-olds was worse.

I will also spare you the first poems of my second career, which forty-six years later I am still pursuing, but I should tell you that they resembled the work of Stephen Crane, which I had just discovered and which I believed to be the most extraordinary literature ever created. I had read great portions of

From the *Threepenny Review*, "Beauty and/or Truth," (winter 1994).

the Old Testament in the King James Version, I had read *MacBeth, Hamlet,* and *The Merchant of Venice,* I had read Edgar Allan Poe, Longfellow, and Bryant, as well as two poems by Milton, the syntax of which completely baffled me. Except for the Bible, which was forced on me by my Hebrew teacher, I had read all this at the insistence of various high school teachers, and none of it had meant a thing to me. I had even memorized the first twenty-some lines of *The Canterbury Tales,* recited them in my ninth-grade English class, and taken my seat and fought to stay awake while the other recitations droned on. In my final semester of high school, I had read Wilfred Owen and had been dazzled to discover I was not the only young man who feared and hated war. However, Owen's work was so complex in its structure it did not tempt me toward imitation as Crane's work did.

In the Desert

In the desert
I saw a creature, naked, bestial,
Who, squatting upon the ground,
Held his heart in his hands,
And ate of it.
I said: "Is it good, friend?"
"It is bitter—bitter," he answered;
"But I like it
Because it is bitter,
And because it is my heart."

Fifteen minutes after reading the Crane poem, I was busy scribbling the first poem of this second career.

Later that evening I showed my poem to my twin brother, Eddie, who immediately pronounced it a work of original genius. (He had not yet read Stephen Crane.) The next day I embarked on an imitation of "I saw a man pursuing the horizon," which also captivated Edward. I can't recall where I'd found the Crane poems; they were not in the anthology I'd purchased for my Introduction to Literature class, taught by a gentle and very generous woman named Mrs. Goldman, whose husband was also a poet. We had started with fiction, and I'd come across the Crane while taking a short break from *A Passage to India,* a book whose characters I had trouble keeping straight. One reading of Crane and I was undone.

I no longer recall why within a week I tired of writing like Stephen Crane. Perhaps Edward grew bored with the sameness of my verses. More likely it was caused by my growing awareness that I scarcely believed what I was writing, for in truth my heart was not bitter, I had never been to the desert, nor had I pursued the horizon. In a curious way I realized that the poems of my first career had been more satisfying to create, for they were large, expansive, and full of a powerful yearning for union with the rain, the wind, with growing things, and ultimately with other people.

෯

The poems of that first career had been more satisfying for another reason, one more difficult to define. They had stunned me with their presence when they leaped out of my mouth, for they possessed a "voice" I had not known was mine. When quite suddenly while walking alone at night I enunciated the words, "We are one with the rain," I did not enunciate the words in any unusual manner; I'm not speaking of voice in that sense, for in that sense it was my ordinary, daytime voice. What startled me was my need to be saying such things, and the immediate satisfaction it gave me to speak them. What I said I would not have spoken to any single person, not even my own twin brother; this was a voice I addressed only to myself and the world as a whole, for I believed the world was listening.

How did this voice differ from what I might call my ordinary, daily voice? Its vocabulary was clearly different, its vocabulary and its tone, for it was always serious, as I was not in ordinary conversation, and it lacked the practicality of what I commonly said. For example, at fourteen I might have said to a larger or older boy I was hoping to placate or scare off, "Go take a flying fuck at a rolling doughnut," a remark that passed for humor in my junior high school. While my poetic voice would welcome the alliteration of *flying fuck* and the internal rhyme of *rolling doughnut,* it had no room yet for what I considered vulgarity, wit—stale or otherwise—and the unlikely image of that rolling doughnut. The new voice accepted the commonplace only when it kept its dignity; thus it could say "underfoot I hear the shards of last year's leaves," and it would have welcomed "drop by soft drop the rain smears the breath of elms."

I do not mean to suggest that this new voice was ignorant or in hiding; it knew perfectly well that my other voice could say "flying fuck," but it didn't care. In fact, it knew everything I knew including a great deal I hadn't known I knew, and thus listening to it I began to sense who I was or was becoming. It was a little frightening to learn suddenly that I was a person who cared for the world far more than he could admit to anyone, a person who possessed a voice so vulnerable to the shock of its own emotions it could reveal itself only in darkness and solitude.

In "Vox Humana," a brilliant early poem by Thom Gunn (a name that meant nothing to me at age fourteen), the voice of the poem concludes by addressing the self thusly:

> Or if you call me the blur
> that in fact I am, you shall
> yourself remain blurred, hanging
> like smoke indoors. For you bring,
> to what you define now, all
> there is, ever, of future.

Lacking the tools to write true poetry at age fourteen, I was nonetheless beginning to discover, define, and accept my moral self. Without knowing it, I had begun to create my future.

❧

Back to my second career. Within a few days of tiring of Stephen Crane I had discovered a far more satisfying model: "The Preludes" of T. S. Eliot. Rereading them now in my wife's copy of the same anthology I used in college, where I first found them, I find she has written "4 miniature paintings" just above the text. (She had a sharp eye for detail even then.) I can still recall what attracted me to them; they concern the lives of individuals in a modern city, and their feelings for the difficulties of those lives struck me as similar to my own, only more profound:

> You had such a vision of the street
> As the street hardly understands;
> Sitting along the bed's edge, where
> You curled the paper from your hair,
> Or clasped the yellow soles of feet
> In the palms of both soiled hands.

That woman could be my mother, I thought, rising for work in the dark, as she did morning after morning. She could be the young woman next door beside whom I stood waiting for the bus on Seven Mile Road to take her downtown to her job as a stenographer and me to my early morning class. On especially cold mornings we would come almost face to face to share whatever warmth there was, but usually she seemed unaware of my presence, lost in thought, her dark hair tumbling over the fake fur collar of her black coat, her pale, finely chiseled features fixed in an expression I could not fathom. Suddenly I thought, I know her mind, she has divined "The conscience of a blackened street / Impatient to assume the world," she is yearning for the presence "of some infinitely gentle / Infinitely suffering thing." I had for some time harbored a kind of love for her, and now I realized in a flash she was who I would be if I had been a woman, and she was the woman Eliot had created.

Writing under the discipleship of Eliot proved far more difficult than copying Crane. For one thing, it demanded I open my eyes to the city around me and to those who shared it with me. The poems could no longer exist in a landscape without time or particularity. There were also new formal demands, for this was a poetry of great rhythmic control and subtlety, and the rhyming was never forced. Poetry modeled after Eliot did not simply gush out of me while I played Ravel or Holst on the Victrola. The whole process took on a new dimension; instead of writing for twenty minutes and getting twenty lines, I was working for hours and getting only fragments of four or five lines I could tolerate.

Meanwhile, in class Mrs. Goldman turned our attention to "The Love Song of J. Alfred Prufrock." She was kind and learned enough to translate the epigraph from Dante and relate it to the poem's theme. I was slightly distressed by the poet's insistence on showing off his Italian, but the poem's opening captivated me: "Let us go then, you and I . . ." I had no doubt that the "I" was anyone who read the poem, in this case the young Wayne University poet. I loved the sudden shifts of focus, the dizzying moves from one locale to another, for the art I knew best was that of the movies. Since forging transitions between the little four-line hunks I'd been writing was giving me fits, it occurred to me that if Eliot could get away without them, so could Levine. While it became obvious that parts of the world of his city were totally foreign to me— "And would it have been worth it, after all, / After the cups, the marmalade, the tea, / Among the porcelain"—I still felt a powerful kinship with the poet. I believed that T. S. Eliot was who I might have been had I been older, wiser, far better educated, and a genius.

One day before the semester ended a very feisty, curly-haired little guy I'd gone to high school with, Jerome, asked Mrs. Goldman if the class could look at Eliot's "Gerontion." Mrs. Goldman blanched a moment and said she'd rather not. It was not one of her favorites, it was very complex, and we had to be moving on toward the present, toward the lyricism of Dylan Thomas. Jerome hung tough.

"Mrs. Goldman," he said, "I'm glad to hear you say it's not one of your favorites, but I'd like you to explain a couple lines," and he began to read:

> My house is a decayed house,
> And the jew squats on the window sill, the owner,
> Spawned in some estaminet of Antwerp,
> Blistered in Brussels, patched and peeled in London.

When he stopped reading, he looked up at Mrs. Goldman and said, "The jew doesn't even get a capital letter."

"What is an 'estaminet'?" someone asked.

"It's really a French word," Mrs. Goldman said. "It means a small café."

Jerome, who was Jewish, interjected, "My father said he thought it meant a brothel."

"Yes," Mrs. Goldman said, braving it, "it could very well mean a whorehouse."

"What do you think of it?" said Jerome, "this poetry by the great T. S. Eliot?"

"I hate it," she said.

On the way home after school I stopped at our local branch library and there located the little black *Collected Poems, 1909–1935*. After dinner, alone in my room, I discovered "Burbank with a Baedeker: Bleistein with a Cigar":

> But this or such was Bleistein's way:
> A saggy bending of the knees
> And elbows, with the palms turned out,
> Chicago Semite Viennese.
>
> A lusterless protrusive eye
> Stares from the protozoic slime
> At a perspective of Canaletto.
> The smokey candle end of time
>
> Declines. On the Rialto once.
> The rats are underneath the piles.
> The jew is underneath the lot . . .

ॐ

Anti-Semitism, the hatred of the Jew, is part of who I am. I did not know such a thing existed until I was five years old, in kindergarten, and returning home one day a girl no older than I informed me that I was nothing but a dirty Jew, a Christ-killer, and I deserved everything I got. Home, I asked my mother what all this was about; she gazed upward for the strength to begin to define for me the world I was to grow up in. She explained that Christ, Jesus Christ, was a man who had lived two thousand years before in Palestine; many people took him as their God or the prophet of their God, and they claimed the Jews, which were who we were, had killed him.

"Did we kill him?" I said.

"No," my mother said, "but that won't stop them from saying it."

I wish I had known then what was so fully documented by the PBS program "The Longest Hatred": you don't need Jews to have anti-Semitism. In areas of Poland where Jews no longer exist, they are blamed for every conceivable social ill. Like any Jew of my era growing up in non-Jewish neighborhoods, I could go on for hours recounting examples of personal insult and discrimination, but I will neither bore you nor horrify you. In a recent poem entitled "The Old Testament," I wrote the following when describing myself at age thirteen:

> I remember putting myself to sleep dreaming
> of the tomatoes coming into fullness, the pansies
> laughing in the spring winds, the magical wisteria
> climbing along the garage, and dreaming of Hitler,
> of firing a single shot from a foot away, one
> that would tear his face into a caricature of mine,
> tear stained, bloodied, begging for a moment's peace.

If anything, I have understated my desire to kill Hitler. At thirteen I was very small for my age; in fact, I did not come into my growth until unusually late, and even then I did not make it to 5′ 10″. At age sixteen, after receiving a bad beating in the parking lot of a neighborhood theater, I decided to remold myself. I joined a Jewish athletic center where I could lift weights and take boxing instruction from a great amateur fighter. I looked for work that was physically demanding so that my body could grow larger and more powerful. I resorted to the use of my fists when I was provoked. This was totally against my nature, which was contemplative and retiring. In other words, without knowing it, I had internalized the image of me that a hostile world projected, and I was doing everything within my power to deny it. I had joined the enemy, though I was not to realize this for years.

છ

In the spring of 1953 I had an opportunity to meet T. S. Eliot, who still occupied the role he had when I'd first read him as the greatest living poet writing in English, which in those days for Americans meant the greatest living poet. I was spending some weeks living in Cambridge, Massachusetts, with friends, and had become a frequent visitor of the Grolier Book Shop, which was fewer than a hundred yards from the apartment I shared. Gordon Carnie, the owner of the shop, was a singularly generous man who allowed me to stand or sit and read any book I chose from his enormous stash of poetry. On weekends he even allowed me to take a single book back to my place if I promised to keep it "virgin." One Friday afternoon while I was the only potential customer in the store, Gordon turned to me and asked if I admired the work of T. S. Eliot. I answered that of course I did and briefly described his early influence on me, omitting the Jewish business.

Gordon instructed me to appear at the shop the next afternoon, a Saturday, at precisely three. The store would be closed, the shade lowered on the front door, but I was to knock three times on the glass, and Gordon would let me in. He had known Eliot for ages, and he was sure I would find him utterly wonderful. Gordon handed me a new translation of Lorca's *Gypsy Ballads* to read over the weekend with "white gloves on," and the matter was settled.

In truth, the matter was far from settled. I told no one about the invitation and instead spent a sleepless night wondering what I might do if Eliot were suddenly to blurt out a racist remark. By this time I'd read his lectures delivered at the University of Virginia and published as *After Strange Gods:* they are not only cunningly reactionary, they are openly anti-Semitic. (To the Virginians he says, "You have here, I imagine, at least some recollection of a 'tradition,' such as the influx of foreign populations has almost effaced in some parts of the North." Later he calls for the unity of religious background in the maintenance of an intelligent tradition; thus "reasons of race and religion combine to make any large number of free-thinking Jews undesirable." Although his poems still haunted me with their beauty and power—by this time I'd pored over *The Four Quartets* and found them awesome—I had come to loathe the image I had of the man.) On Saturday I went with some friends to Cape Ann, and when next I saw Gordon nothing was said about my defection. Thus I lost my chance with one of the lords of the English language.

Later when I read Pound's ravings, the transcripts of the radio broadcasts he delivered on behalf of Mussolini, I was far less troubled. I had already been warned what to expect, and curiously I detected no snobbery nor personal animosity in Pound. This was a man gone mad, one who would soon be locked up in a cage for dogs, from which he would write his way back to partial sanity in his "Pisan Cantos." I was also warned regarding Céline and I avoided what I was assured would infuriate me. In *Death on the Installment Plan* I later found one of the literary giants of our time.

❧

Each of us experiences anti-Semitism in his or her own way. I can only record how profound were the changes on my personality it rendered, and, looking back over the years, I can't believe any of them improved me. I didn't need to become physically stronger; my life's work would not consist of loading boxcars onto boxcars. I didn't need to spend hundreds of hours developing a strong left hook and a decent jab. I still recall my brother Eddie's motto when the war ended and we discovered how vast had been the assault on our people. "We will not go quietly," he would say to me, by which he meant that if I were worthy of being his brother, I would have to go down fighting. I accepted the challenge. For others growing up in a later and different manner, the world must have been far friendlier. In a piece published in the September 1988 *AWP Newsletter*, the poet Robert Pinsky describes himself telling a Polish audience that for an American of his generation anti-Semitism "could be treated primarily as a matter of manners." Pinsky admits that this "was partly half-conscious bravado." He then gets utterly serious and states that he "declined to be anyone's even potential victim." Robert Pinsky is perhaps twenty years younger than I and grew up in New Jersey and not in Detroit, and it is good to know he was able to avoid what invaded me.

Even for little Levine, it wasn't all a nightmare. By the age of twenty-six I had bulked up to 165 pounds and had gained enough strength to set a weightlifting record at the University of Iowa. Back in Detroit, working out with the real lifters who would go on to their Olympic gold medals at London and Helsinki, I met a sweet, naive country boy from west of Saginaw. He'd come to Detroit for work; he wanted to make money, learn ballroom dancing, buy a new Ford, and return home in triumph. This was before television, and Herb didn't read Dreiser, so it was impossible to divine the source of his inspiration. One afternoon he asked me what I "was." He had seemed to take a liking to me because I was the only person he'd ever met who read lots of books and could explain difficult matters like how we got a constitution or why electricity could kill you. "What am I?" I said, "I'm Jewish."

"No," he said, "I mean what are you, who were your ancestors? When you say you're Jewish you mean you're cheap or you're money hungry, but the real Jewish people were an ancient people who lived in the biblical lands."

"I know who the Jews were," I said, "and I'm one of them. I'm not money hungry. I'm a descendant of Moses and Abraham. I'm a direct descendant of Jacob's son Levi. That's how I got the last name Levine." His mouth fell open. His wide blue eyes bulged. He thrust out one soft hand to shake mine, and so I took his hand. "I sure wouldn't have guessed you'd look like you. Wait until I tell my family I met a real Jewish person. We didn't know you people were still alive." We were still alive and determined to stay that way. Would that Herb had been the worst of those we dealt with.

❧

And now in the spring of 1993 the whole Philip Larkin shit-storm is about to hit the fan here in the United States, the storm that hit England last year with the publication of the Andrew Motion biography and *The Selected Letters,* edited by Anthony Thwaite. "The tone of sour majesty, of sardonic resignation infused with wordless romantic yearning, is something we might call Larkinesque," Edward Hirsch wrote recently. I think that puts very well what most of us would have said just a short time ago. However, reviewing the Motion biography in the *TLS,* Ian Hamilton begins thusly:

A couple of weeks ago, there was an article in the *Independent* about a rap performer called Ice Cube, author of "A Bitch is a Bitch" and "Now I Gotta Wet'cha." Ice Cube, we were told, is notorious for his misogyny and racism and for whipping up his fans into ecstasies of loathing: he has them "grooving to a litany of hate." Only one of Ice Cube's lines was quoted—"You can't trust no bitch. Who can I trust? Me"—but the reviewer did attempt to pinpoint his subject's characteristic manner of address. He called Ice Cube's language "incessantly Larkinesque."

Hamilton goes on to speculate that the readers of the *Independent* were not meant to think of "a somewhat poignant type of artist, wry, subtle, elegiac." By Larkinesque, the reviewer meant Ice Cube "uses the word 'fuck' a lot." You might well ask how we got here so fast; Larkin only died in 1985. For starters, the letters will show him describing his Pakistani neighbor as a "nigger" and explaining that he no longer attended cricket matches because there were "too many fucking niggers about," and in another letter he resorts to capitals to express his need for "WATCHING SCHOOLGIRLS SUCK EACH OTHER OFF WHILE YOU WHIP THEM." As Christopher Hitchens wrote in *Vanity Fair,* "the letters are threaded with every known specimen of bigotry." They are also full of mean-spirited remarks about most of his fellow writers, including some who were his close friends. Example: of his best friend Kingsley Amis he writes, "The only reason I hope to predecease him is that I find it next to impossible to say anything nice about him at his memorial service." He wrote to his friend Barbara Pym that he felt deeply humiliated to live in a country that spent more on education than on defense, and of course he adored Mrs. Thatcher and described the world that was not the U.K. as "filthy abroad." But why go on? Does any of this surprise the lovers of his poetry?

Certainly the poet and critic Tom Paulin could hardly not have guessed much of this. In a piece published in 1990, before the appearance of the letters and the biography, he describes Larkin's "snarl, his populism and his calculated philistinism" as speaking "for that gnarled and angry puritanism which is so deeply ingrained in the culture." Larkin had referred to himself as "one of nature's Orangemen," which Paulin calls a strategy to allow him to "conceal the knowledge that he had created many outstandingly beautiful poems. In that distinctly embarrassed English manner he had to bury his pride in his artistic creations under several sackfuls of ugly prejudices."

The man who wrote, "They fuck you up, your mum and dad," was indeed deeply fucked up, but then he never pretended to be otherwise. When I spoke to the poet Mary Karr, who published a very moving elegy on Larkin, "Post-Larkin Triste," in which she revealed that the one carefully written fan letter she'd written him had been returned unopened, she straightened me out by saying, "He was hardly a moral titan. He was no Keats." She intended to read the letters and the biography and doubted they would change her attitude regarding the fineness of the poems.

If you grew up, as I did, close to racehorses, and fell in love with the beauty and power of the animals and the spectacle of the races, you had to be swept away when you first encountered, as I did in 1957, Larkin's "At Grass," a depiction of two former-fabled racers now in "the cold shade they shelter in." After a description of those distant afternoons on which they made their names famous, the poem brings us back to the present evening:

> Dusk brims the shadows.
> Summer by summer all stole away,
> The starting-gates, the crowds and cries—
> All but the unmolesting meadows.
> Almanacked, their names live; they
>
> Have slipped their names, and stand at ease
> Or gallop for what must be joy,
> And not a fieldglass sees them home,
> Or curious stop-watch prophesies;
> Only the groom, and the groom's boy,
> With bridles in the evening come.

For Paulin "the threatening atmosphere of the closing lines is Larkin's response to modern social democracy." For him the horses "are heroic ancestors—famous generals, perhaps." For me they are race horses, and the poem is a gorgeous and somewhat terrifying account of what it means to slip your name. They are what we will all be when fame or attention deserts us, if we ever had them. As the night comes on, winners and losers are at last equals.

I find it hardest to deal with Larkin on jazz. How could someone who seemed to love that music so deeply go on about "niggers" so often? Even there he did not mask himself entirely, for he made it clear that Charlie Parker was one of the great spoilers of the century, along with Picasso and Pound. In other words, when the music of black Americans became intellectual, for Larkin it ceased being jazz. In his jazz book, *All What Jazz,* he wrote, "the tension between artist and audience in jazz slackened when the Negro stopped wanting to entertain the white man."

What is it about Larkin's poetry that got us? I could seldom teach his work with any success; most of my students found him dreary and gray, and perhaps they—in their youth—were right to see him that way. But there were always a few very bright and "experienced" students who seemed to twig to what was best in his poetry, and they became Larkin lovers for life, or at least until the present storm.

Coming

On longer evenings,
Light, chill and yellow,
Bathes the serene
Foreheads of houses.
A thrush sings,
Laurel-surrounded
In the deep bare garden,
Its fresh-peeled voice
Astonishing the brickwork.
It will be spring soon,
It will be spring soon—
And I, whose childhood
Is a forgotten boredom,
Feel like a child

> Who comes on a scene
> Of adult reconciling,
> And can understand nothing
> But the unusual laughter,
> And starts to be happy.

Every time I read this poem, I think of a phrase from Robert Graves, "nothing promised that is not performed." There is such modesty in the writing, there is such a perfect relationship between what is said and what is left unsaid. And the poem is unafraid to assert its final thrill; spring is coming to England, not to Eden, but to our world that for so long squanders its energies in winter or worse. (One feels Larkin knew all there was to know about winter and worse.) As in the best of Larkin, the language is precise and fresh, exactly like the voice of the thrush "astonishing the brickwork."

No doubt Auden's lines from "In Memory of W. B. Yeats" will be called up in defense of Larkin. As Auden wrote, time may be "indifferent in a week / To a beautiful physique," but I seriously doubt it "worships language and forgives / Everyone by whom it lives." The truth is, time merely passes. As Ellen Bryant Voigt has written, "What Larkin affirms for us—what Hardy affirmed for Larkin—is that great poems require neither the extraordinary life circumstances of Keats or Hikmet . . . , but a relentless 'striving to be accurate' and, sometimes, a certain ruthlessness toward the very sensibility that produces the poem." Larkin's poems remain what they are, but it doesn't not matter that their author was a shit.

ᘓ

A few Saturdays ago, while walking home from the grocery store, my wife suddenly quoted three lines of poetry to me:

> No memory of having starred
> Atones for later disregard,
> Or keeps the end from being hard.

It was late in the day, and our street, which is lined with enormous eucalyptus trees and deodar cedars, was cool and lovely in the stiff breezes that often visit this valley before sunset. Many of the front yards we passed were rich with tulips and violets, which took on a deep purple cast in the shaded light. All day I had been struggling with my feelings regarding the racism of Larkin, and my head was full of poetry and anger. "That's Frost, isn't it?" she said. She recalled the day over thirty years before I'd come home from a reading by Frost at Stanford at which he'd insulted the entire audience. He'd stopped in the middle of "Mending Wall" to scold someone in the audience for his terrible posture, and then claimed his poem had been ruined for him and refused to finish it. No sense of irony there, either. "He was my favorite poet back then," she said. "I think you preferred Stevens and Williams and Hart Crane, but he was my favorite." I asked her if the story changed her attitude. "No," she said, "but later when you told me about his letter to Pound in which he referred to an editor as a 'nigger' and said he'd never have answered the man if he'd known he was a 'nigger,' then I had real trouble reading him." By this time we'd reached our house. I thought the conversation was at an end, but when we sat down to dinner an hour later, she turned to me and said, "I want someone who writes that well to be exemplary." She had in mind both Frost and Larkin. I asked why they should be better than anyone else. She didn't answer at first, but it became clear she was formulating an answer. Finally she said, "Because they were given a gift. I know poets work hard at their craft, but the gift, which is so enormous, they did nothing to earn. They should be exemplary."

During dinner Fran recalled that Cesar Chavez had died the night before. We agreed that he was the greatest person to emerge from this valley, perhaps the greatest Californian of the century. I'd seen him only twice, on marches I'd taken here and in Sacramento. I'd been struck by the intensity of the man and how it contrasted with the gentleness of his voice and gestures. I thought that time in Sacramento: there is someone I could love and follow. When some months later I mentioned my feelings to someone I knew was older and thought was wiser, Kenneth Rexroth, Kenneth laughed at me and replied,

"He's a great union organizer, but he's just a politician." Although I felt foolish, I didn't change my attitude.

After dinner we watched part of a Burt Lancaster movie on television; when it became clear good looks and virtue would triumph, we turned it off and went to bed. Lying in the dark, I asked myself the question I had not asked my wife: was I an exemplary person? Some questions are too stupid to merit an answer, so I got the answer I deserved, silence. Did the fact I never received the gift of a Frost or a Larkin excuse me from leading an exemplary life? Silence. The truth was astonishingly simple: I agreed with my wife. People with such gifts should lead exemplary lives, but they don't, and though at age nineteen I discovered the meanness of spirit of Eliot, I still expect them to. It wasn't a question of forgiving Eliot or Larkin, for no one had asked for my forgiveness. They were snobbish shits, and Pound and Céline were raving lunatics, but when they wrote at their best I seemed not to care about their extracurricular behavior. The poems have their lives, and I have mine, forty-six years of which seem to have taught me nothing.

Larry Levis

Hearing of the death of Larry Levis this past May, Jane Cooper, one of my oldest and surely my dearest friend in poetry, wrote me a consoling letter, one that touched me deeply and helped as much as such letters can. "I think this must almost be like losing a son for you," she wrote. Perhaps once, thirty years ago when I first met Larry and got to know and love him, I might have thought of him as a son, but it was not long before we became simply friends and brothers in the impossible art of poetry. What many who knew us well failed to realize was that I took from Larry, from his advice and from the poems he wrote, more than I ever gave to him. It was easy to take from Larry, for his whole vision of why we are here on this earth had to do with giving. One sees it clearly in a little essay he wrote about teachers who mattered and didn't matter to him: "to try to conserve one's energy for some later use, to try to teach as if one isn't quite there and has more important things to do, is a way, quite simply, of betraying oneself."

In this same letter Jane goes on to describe the year she spent at Iowa teaching along with Larry. "There was a gentle mysteriousness about him then which was very attractive but which at the time I respected as a kind of boundary." Amazingly, without believing she knew him well, Jane put her finger precisely on a quality of his presence I could not have articulated, for from the moment I met him Larry struck me as that rare person who knows exactly who he is and finds the mere fact of his particular existence both just and incredibly funny, cosmically—if you will—riotously funny. That a ranch boy from Selma, California, the raisin capital of the universe, "a

From *American Poet*, "Larry Levis" (fall 1996).

kind of teenage failure, an unathletic, acne-riddled virgin who owned the slowest car in town, a 1959 Plymouth sedan that had fins like irrelevant twin sharks rising above the taillights," should at age sixteen decide to become a poet always struck him as both outrageous and perfectly right. He tells us in a brilliant and hilarious autobiographical essay that the decision was made on the basis of one line in a single poem, all the other lines of which were awful. As a junior at Selma High he had been reading Eliot, Stevens, and Frost on his own and decided he would try to write a poem. He did this one night in his bedroom, turned out the light, and told himself that if in the morning he found one good line he would try to become a poet. And then he took back *try*. "You will either be a poet," he told himself, "and become a better and better one, or you will not be a poet." The next morning he found in the awful poem that one good line. "All the important decisions were made in that moment."

From the moment I met Larry I was aware of that gentle mysteriousness that Jane wrote of. In mid-September 1964 this tall, slender, loose-limbed, country boy entered my office at Fresno State and asked if we might discuss the possibility of his taking my beginning poetry writing class even though he was only an entering freshman and lacked all the prerequisites. I asked him to take a seat, and he did so, sprawling in a chair before me, and then he asked permission to smoke, which—being a smoker myself—I granted. I described the course to him, the fact I required the students to write poems in specific forms before they were released to the chaos of free verse, which by then they might discover was not so free after all. He smiled and nodded his approval. I wondered had he read any modern poetry, for the experience might be a richer one for him if he had. "Oh, yes," he said, he'd been reading Eliot, Frost, and Stevens for two years now. He still had trouble with some of Stevens. At the moment he was struggling with Hart Crane and Rimbaud. He wondered if I might help him understand some of Rimbaud. Not knowing French, I couldn't, but perhaps I could help him with Crane. He collected himself and rose and began to walk slowly around my small office, his mouth fixed, nodding his head up and down. A minute passed or perhaps what seemed like a minute during which he was seriously thinking, and then he leaned back against an empty desk across from mine with his arms fully extended, a stance I would become familiar with as the years passed. He looked me full in the face, his dark eyes under long lashes staring into mine, and I was for the first time struck by his physical beauty, of which he seemed totally unaware. "Might I enroll in your class?" he said. "I believe it is exactly what I want." At that moment I knew without the least doubt that the coming semester would be a triumph.

And a triumph it was. It was probably the best class I was ever privileged to be a part of, for week after week Larry presented us with poems. They were not perfect poems, sometimes they were not even good poems, but they were always poems. Imagine getting this description of a small-town pharmacy from an eighteen-year-old beginner six weeks into his first college semester:

> In the town of 20 pool cues
> of noses broken over the feel of pussy,
> among the bottles of grease and candy
> lining the shelves,
> the men laughed,
> they stole cars and left them in ditches, smouldering.
> Their wives, spitting at irons, never looked up.
> They grew older.
>
> —(From "The Town")

He may have hated Selma. ("You could die in a town like that without lifting a finger.") But he was already Selma's one poet. The true miracle of that semester was not, astonishingly enough, the poems Larry handed in; it was what happened to five other students, for they too sensed someone rare and remarkable was in their midst. These five caught fire from Larry and from his poems and began to write utterly surprising things that struggled with the agony and humor of coming of age in the little valley towns that gave birth to them. This was my seventh year of teaching creative writing, but it was the first time I discovered how much one genius can give to those around him or her when that genius has an un-quenchable need to give.

I received a sabbatical that semester, and my wife and I decided to try Spain for the following year. In late August, the night before we left, there was a quiet knock on the door, and when I answered it Larry stood shyly there in the ferocious heat with a six-pack in hand and asked if it was okay for him to come in and say good-bye. I welcomed him into the heat of our un-air-conditioned house. The kids were in bed, and all the living room furniture—save for one kitchen chair—had been stowed in a back bedroom so that the family renting our house could enjoy their own possessions. The place looked like a venue for a Ping-Pong tournament. I offered Larry the one chair, and he sat upright before my wife and me, who sat cross-legged before him. After some minutes of stilted con-versation, the three of us finally exploded with laughter at the stupidity of this arrangement, and for half an hour we swapped places as Larry entertained us with a series of won-derful riffs on the theme of the one chair. When in full flight he was the funniest man I have ever known, for his humor was totally spontaneous and always took off from the elements at hand the way a jazz musician might walk out into a series of variations on a musical theme.

By this time Larry had written several of the poems that appear in his first book, *Wrecking Crew,* which won the 1971 U.S. Award of the International Poetry Forum and was pub-lished by Pitt the next year. Those poems were written in his late teens and early twenties and give only a hint of the power to come. His second book, *The Afterlife,* which won the 1976 Lamont Award, shows the expanding range of his fascinations and his style. In the stunning long poem "Linnets"—written when he was twenty-eight—one hears for the first time the voice that is distinctively Levis.

> ONE morning with a 12 gauge my brother shot
> what he said was a linnet. He did this at close range
> where it sang on a flowering almond branch. Any-
> one could have done the same and shrugged it off,
> but my brother joked about it for days, describing

> how nothing remained of it, how he watched for
> feathers and counted only two gold ones which he
> slipped behind his ear. He grew uneasy and care-
> less; nothing remained. He wore loud ties and two
> tone shoes. He sold shoes. He sold soap. Nothing
> remained. He drove on the roads with a little hole
> in the air behind him.

By this time he'd earned an M.A. degree from Syracuse, where he worked with Donald Justice, and a PhD from Iowa, where with the help of his friend the Mexican poet Ernesto Trejo he explored the great twentieth-century poetry in Spanish. By this time certainly he was no longer a son to me. Indeed he had come into himself. Or perhaps I should say he had created himself, the self of which he would later write: "driving a tractor, furrowing out a vineyard of muscats for my father one day, I was for some reason immediately impressed by how lucky I was to have been born at all, especially to be born as a human being rather than, as I wrote later in a poem, 'a horse, or a gnat.'" This was the Larry Levis to whom I mailed my new work each month—if there were work to send. He would return my poems with praise when they merited it and something else when they didn't, and I tried my best to do the same for him with an equal measure of tact and honesty.

Looking back now, I can see that it was during my first year in Spain that my relationship with Larry began to change, for that was the first year of what became the crucial correspondence of my life. I was the only American poet I knew within driving distance, and so when Larry first sent me a poem for my approval or criticism I answered with one of my own. I had learned even during that first year as his teacher how sensitively and shrewdly he could read poetry, but it was only in the letters I discovered what a resourceful and brilliant practical critic he was, and as the years passed I grew more and more to need him in more ways than I can describe. I heard of Larry's death in Athens, Ohio, where I was scheduled to give a poetry reading within a few hours. My hosts, knowing of my loss, were extraordinarily considerate. The meaning of Larry's death had not begun to dawn on me, and by putting it on hold—simply by refusing to believe it—I was able to read. At a certain point in the reading I faltered, for I realized that the very lines I was reading were lines Larry had either given me or urged me to write in order to rescue a poem. The first time this happened I was able to pass over it with only a word to myself, but when a few minutes later I entered the conclusion of a poem I had years before struggled with I realized these final lines I was reading were lines designed by Larry. I had to stop and tell the audience what I had to tell myself, that my brother in poetry, my dear friend, had died and that I owed the lines I had just read to Larry Levis. I did not tell them that for thirty years his fierce devotion to his art had served as my inspiration and model. I did not tell them that I found in his poetry an originality and daring that urged me to risk more in my own writing. I did not tell them that when I am weary of the mediocrity and smallness of so much that passes for poetry I go to Larry's work and revive my belief in the value of the art we shared.

No, I never told Larry that either, nor did I tell him that I thought he had become the finest poet of his generation and probably a better poet than his old teacher. I wouldn't have dared, for he would have shambled about the room, bobbing his head up and down, and then gone off on a series of wonderful riffs on a theme such as "the most embarrassing things ever said in Fresno," or "why it is important not to drink after dark" or "how vitamin deficiency turned Levine into Edgar Guest." *The Dollmaker's Ghost, Winter Stars,* and *The Widening Spell of the Leaves,* his last three books, are collections of poetry that will last as long as our language survives, and it's likely that my greatest contribution to literature is the small part I played in creating them.

Craft Non-Lecture

This craft non-lecture has a curious history, which requires a little background if it is to make sense. I wrote a lecture on the state of our poetry to be delivered in Iowa City earlier this year; the audience would have been a large collection of poetry brats and elder statespersons, people who took themselves with great seriousness and were very assured about their position in poetry. It was meant to startle and insult; it was very abrasive. I was leaving town the next day and thus felt confident I could escape before harm was done to me. Due to a breakdown in the sound system in the huge room where I was to deliver the thing, I never had a chance to give it, so I saved it for another opportunity, which came a few weeks later when I went to a writing conference in Alaska. My craft lecture was scheduled on the third day of a ten-day conference, so I would have had to live with these people for a week after insulting them. Within a few hours I could see they were a very different audience. The students, or whatever you call writers who enroll in a summer writing thing, were unknowns; many were rank beginners. I quickly realized my lecture would never do when a woman who'd asked me if I'd ever taken a class in poetry writing gave me a blank stare when I answered that I had and with John Berryman. "John Berrywho?" she said.

The day before I was to give my talk, I was wandering around the campus when a sudden downpour caught me. I shall not bore you with the history of my neurotic dread of wet feet. At any rate, I ran into a building where, to my disgust, I discovered a fiction panel was taking place. The lobby was cold and forbidding; the lecture hall cozy and

From the *Missouri Review*, "Craft Non-Lecture," 1987.

warm, and my feet would surely dry and I could nap. I did not nap. For some reason I became very attentive to this panel, for the members seemed to be responding very acutely to questions from the audience, which involved that subject upon which nothing, I believed, useful could be said, the craft of writing. I realized that while I agreed with much that was said I had my own answers to the questions, but I was too polite to correct the panelists before their students. What you will hear now are my responses to the questions and to the answers given by Bobbie Ann Mason, Ntozake Shange, and Nancy Willard—so when you hear those names they should not startle you. Or puzzle you.

I should begin by making it clear I have an antipathy to the notion of a craft lecture, that is, to the notion that I have some methodology that I can pass on to you, perhaps even to the notion that there is a craft. For certain I don't believe I can pass on to you what I've learned in forty years of fooling around with words. People ask me, Do you write in the evening or the morning? as though my answer will be useful for them, as though the things that worked for a man of fifty-eight who hopes to forget most of what he's written will work for someone twenty-two who yearns to write most of what he or she has already read. I have learned and unlearned a great deal in these years, and because I've unlearned so much—finding that what I once believed was useless—I'm somewhat loath to set down any rules of the game. If you're around long enough, you tend to discover how foolish you have been, and if you discover enough times how foolish you have been, it dawns on you that you are undoubtedly foolish now. It's possible I have another reason for not wanting to address the question of craft, and this will require a small anecdote. Some years ago I was involved in a doubles match in which one of my opponents was a great tennis player and the other hopeless. The great player, a former Chilean Junior Davis Cup star, was the teacher of the hopeless player. The star hit a shot none of us had ever hit before, a top-spin lob; it was a perfect winner. His partner and pupil said, "How did you do that?" He didn't answer. The guy asked again and again got no answer. He said, "I pay you twenty-five bucks an hour so you *won't* tell me how you hit certain shots. This is ridiculous." The Chilean pro called us all to the net, and he said to me, "You are a teacher of poetry, right?" "Yes," I said. "Do you teach your students everything you know, or do you keep back a little for yourself?" He was, I think, right, perhaps I do keep back a little for myself. You never know when you're going to need it.

I could of course begin by recommending Aristotle's *Poetics,* for they are in their way a craft lecture and a great one. Observe the unities of time, space, and action. Start as near to the conclusion as possible so that stage time will most closely resemble actual time. Keep unseemly events off stage, and in this way what you will write will never resemble films or television dreck, and you will never become a popular writer. If you're going to kill someone in a poem, don't describe the bullet going in or the poison taking effect right down to the last shivering of the eyelids and the flow of gore. Once you get in competition with movies you're going to lose. Keep the screwing offstage in the poem; you can't begin to compete with what they have. They know postures you've never dreamed of, postures that require world-class athletes to execute. You can't get that into your poem, so keep it offstage.

Listening to the fiction panel, I was struck by how perfectly valid and in disagreement their responses to certain questions were. Ntozake Shange said she read her poems and stories, the ones she had doubts about, publicly to get a response from others and also to hear them herself as others might. Bobbie Ann Mason does not live in a community of writers or a community that seems much to care about writing and therefore does not show her work to anyone. Nancy Willard uses her husband, whose ability to read with insight she trusts. A sort of paradigm of possibilities: the large group, the small group— of one, in this case—and no group at all. What worked for them might work for you. And again it might not. We know that Chekhov and D. H. Lawrence could write anywhere and under almost any circumstances; neither had the least trouble with others in the room, and in Chekhov's case, for all he cared, the others could be engaging in conversation or partying, as we now put it. Lawrence could scarcely stop himself from writing; he could not not write.

Mostly I write in a closed room; it's not a prison cell, for it has windows that look out on a garden in one direction and a garage in the other. No spectacular view. Auden said that only maniacs could write with a spectacular view at hand; he mentioned Hitler by name. I was once loaned an apartment high above Sausalito, which possessed a spectacular view of San Francisco; I tried writing there for a few weeks and got nothing, so I went down to the basement and wrote looking out of a window that faced upon the trunk of a massive oak that hid everything else. Here I worked. Upstairs I had wondered why I was sitting alone and lonely; in the basement the imagination brought me company. We know that Keats would take his weekly bath and dress in his best clothes and sit down alone on Saturday night to work on his poems. That's my favorite story of how one should prepare oneself to write. I myself use a lemon-scented bath, or did until it attracted too much attention. (I think people thought I smelled like a gin and tonic; I couldn't get rid of them.)

Hemingway stood up when working on serious fiction. I saw the room in which Emily Dickinson wrote her poems; she sat on a very uncomfortable hassock and worked in short, intense bouts. I even sat on the hassock, but all I could do was recite, "I heard a fly buzz. . . ." She had a very different nature from mine; she envisioned a Protestant deity looking down at her as she worked, and she felt obliged to be uncomfortable. I have no problem with being comfortable and can write lolling in a big overstuffed chair or even in bed. Debt seemed to stimulate Dostoyevsky's imagination. Simmons tells us that in order to meet gambling debts he wrote *The Gambler* in less than a month, that in fact he dictated it and then married the stenographer. So one could take up serious gambling as he did or simply overindulge on credit buying.

But why am I mentioning these writers—Dickinson, Keats, Lawrence, Chekhov, Dostoyevsky? Why go to a genius to get advice? What have they got to do with us, who are, after all, merely humble workers in the fields of writing, harvesting onions and an occasional lemon.

Nancy Willard has said that she let an ending of a novel or short story find her rather than allowing the conscious mind to strain after it. She even gave us hints as to how she might initiate that process: rhythmic activity in which the mind is freed: gardening, washing the floor, perhaps just "walking dully along," to quote Auden. I jog for my health, and in all those hundreds of hours and God knows how many miles I've gotten one poem. But of course I'm still alive, so there may have been other benefits. Largely what my mind is about when I'm jogging is telling me how awful this activity is. It keeps asking me why I am not back home in the lemon-scented hot tub where I belong, with all my dear friends. I think Nancy is right and that my problem is that I haven't found the rhythmic activity that would work for me. Shange mentioned that she would take a nap when she hit an impasse in her writing. This has worked for me. But I have also found while working on particularly boring poems that I simply craved sleep and that need for sleep was perhaps the finest critical sense within me.

Yes, I am that fool who wakes up in the middle of the night believing he has something to write. Shange was very clear that one should not at these moments talk to anyone; by this I think she meant that one should not let other practical concerns break in upon this fit of creativity. I would say, "Yes, don't talk to anyone," or "No, talk to someone, maybe talk to many people." I practiced the "don't talk to anyone" mode for years, and it worked; then I tried the other, and it worked also. In a book about Giacommetti, Michael Lord describes the creative process as it acts itself out through Giacommetti. He was invited by Giacommetti to sit for him, and if you know his painting you know he used very few models. Lord, who was a devotee of Giacommetti, was flattered to be asked to sit and also eager to be of use. Who wouldn't be pleased to be preserved forever in the painting of a great artist? The first day Giacommetti worked very hard and got a lot of the painting, or so Lord believed. When he came back to sit the second day most of what had been painted the first day had been removed. This process went on for several days. Lord had a life he had to get back to, a family in the States, but Alberto kept after him to stay until the painting was finished. So day after day, he allowed himself to be kept modeling. Finally one day he arrived to find Giacommetti not particularly interested in painting at all, or so it seemed. They went out to a café and had coffee, they stayed and had a sandwich, some wine, Alberto talked to his friends. A few hours later they returned to the studio, Giacommetti got down to work, and by that evening he had something he was as satisfied with as he would ever be. When I read that I was thunderstruck. There was no explanation in the book of what had taken place, so I explained it to myself. Giacommetti knew that day that he was inspired, as all of us know when we are inspired after we have practiced a craft or art long enough. Because he was a mature artist and totally confident of his art, he could take that ennoblement, that sense of wholeness that is inspiration, he could take that out of the studio and touch as many elements of his life as possible—the café, the café owner, his buddies, casual acquaintances and dearest friends. He could make his daily rounds and bless each one of his usual stops with that extraordinary condition that he was in, that condition in which you feel you are somebody else, someone larger than you, because you are inspired. In fact you are not somebody else. You are yourself and fully, perhaps for the first time in months, and you merely don't recognize yourself.

Artists used to pray to the muses for that portion of the self that was outside oneself—it felt so foreign they assumed it was. Keats and Coleridge both tell us they were seized by something outside themselves and wrote better than they could. I think they were wrong; I think they were themselves the way we so rarely are. I'm with Giacommetti. I'll stop in the middle and go out into the streets, talk to others (not, of course, about what I'm writing), and see if I can bring back what I see and hear to include it in the poem and somehow enlarge what I'm writing. This process has its risks and its rewards. In extending this sense of well-being one could lose the poem, but one could also enlarge and extend it at the same time, as one touched one's daily life with this rare and mysterious condition. And one could triumph over the fear of losing a poem. I would not recommend this tack for someone nineteen years old; losing a poem at that age can be traumatic.

I don't give a damn about losing one poem. I have books of

poems. I have unpublished books of poems, many of them unworthy of publication. If you're a young poet with nine poems you love, the tenth poem becomes 10 percent of your *oeuvre*. I have no interest in writing another mediocre poem. I have dozens of mediocre poems. I want to write ten more great poems to go with the ten I've already written, so the risk taking is fine for me. Shange also said, "Don't throw anything away. You'll find a use for it." She's young, and she has no idea what will happen if you don't throw things away. All that stuff will crowd you out. You'll wind up like William Saroyan owning two identical houses side by side, one to live in and one to store all the crap he couldn't throw away.

And get it out of your mind. Absolutely remove all this from your mind. Robert Duncan once told me he wanted to develop a college course that would remove things from people's minds so that there would be room for new things or even old and interesting things. One might junk all the sermons one has ever heard, all the advice from one's elders and betters, all the patriotic rubbish and racist tripe one derived from the movies, one might even begin to remove the influence of Rilke from American poetry, so we might stop urging people to change their lives and begin thinking seriously about how we could change our own. Think of merely shedding all the Saturday morning cartoons that kids watch. Last year I was in the locker room at Tufts University—a very expensive school, very difficult to get into, supposedly a very superior school—and as I was preparing to jog, I caught two cultured voices coming from another row of lockers. One said to the other, "Did you see 'The Three Stooges' this morning? They were fabulous." And the other answered, "'The Three Stooges,' damn, I didn't know they were on this morning!" The voice was mournful with loss. I am with Duncan. Clear the decks for action.

Nancy's notion that the ending will find you seems useful. I believe that what that implies is trust the imagination, which I've found to be the hardest advice for young writers to take. Imagine for a moment that I am not Philip Levine. I am instead a highly rational, incredibly intelligent, superbly well-educated poet. I am W. H. Auden at my age. I write about ten poems a year, for more would be unseemly and tasteless in a man of my accomplishments. It's mid-August, and I haven't written a word since June. I think, This will never do. I go directly to the typewriter and command myself to be articulate, candid, and direct. I write, "It has been sixty days since I took seriously / The task of mining the harried brain and evolving Soul / Since I considered the burgeoning summer's toll. . . ." I'm on my way to another mediocre poem, like most of W. H. Auden's late poems. Why? Not because I lack talent. I am W. H. Auden, I have much more talent than Philip Levine, and everyone knows how much smarter I am than that bozo. Let us liken old Auden to a battleship; up there on the bridge is Captain Brain telling all the other parts of the ship how to behave so as to complete this mission, but when one is writing a poem one is not up on the bridge. One is somewhere down in the engine room, stoking the fires, hoping that the ship is not merely going around and around in meaningless circles. It's going to take an especially fortunate combination of winds and sea currents to get us into port, that port called "Ode to a Nightingale," "In the Waiting Room," or "Song of Myself." Let the brain take charge and command the ship and you'll get nowhere someone hasn't been before, for the rational intelligence can easily give you poems already written, especially—as in the case of Auden—poems already written by you. But if you're going somewhere new and undiscovered you have to trust the imagination, you have to truly believe the poem knows better than you and thus follow where it leads.

This is exactly what Lawrence is telling us when, in the essay "Why Fiction Matters," he tells us to trust the novel and not the novelist. He means just this, trust that aspect of the self that creates. Listen to the poem, the tale, you'll hear where it is alive and where it is dead, and follow where the living lines lead. In practical terms, "trust the imagination," which we may repeat without believing or understanding, means that most often what we intend to write when we sit down to write is horseshit, but what we actually write might very well be the real thing. We must be alive to what we are writing and not what we thought we ought to write. "Trust the novel and not the novelist," says Lawrence, meaning trust that man or woman when he or she is generously creative; on other occasions they're ordinary. We know from his notebooks that Dostoyevsky did not want *The Brothers K* to take the direction it did; he wanted Alyosha to dominate the book, but he made him a bore and his disbelieving, half-devil brother utterly fascinating. The book does not reaffirm all the orthodox cant he intended to affirm; instead it's full of deep human anger and doubt. He let it go where it had to go, and we have a great novel. Lawrence tells us that in fiction we discover how people truly are toward each other; we do not have to be critics to know when the scene fails, the dialogue goes hollow, and the writing is forced. What do you do when the poem goes dead? You go back down into the engine room, and you get it. Or you don't get it. You can fail. Failing is no big deal, failing is what we largely do when we live, and, when we live as long as I have and write as much as I, we do a lot of failing.

I've taught at a great many schools, taught poetry writing now for twenty-five years at Fresno State, Brown, Princeton, NYU, Columbia, Vassar, UC Berkeley, the University of Alabama at Birmingham, Tufts, and from all that experience I've learned something remarkable. The best student poets I've encountered were not at Tufts or Princeton or Brown; they were at Fresno State and UAB, the two lousiest schools I've taught at. The worst poetry writing students were at Princeton. This was no accident, and in fact there's a very simple explanation. The students at Fresno State had failed at just about everything; that's why they were at Fresno. If they'd been lucky enough to have wealthy parents, they'd have gone to Stanford; if they'd been academically successful, they'd have gone to UC Berkeley. But they'd lost on both counts, and so they were at this dump. My students at Princeton, Tufts, and Brown had never failed in the academic setting; they had no experience with failure. So when you look at the young Princeton bard's poems and say as politely as you can, this is vomit, he or she goes directly into shock. They sometimes actually weep, right there in class. We know that everyone who tries to write poems fails at first: Keats failed, Rilke failed, Hart Crane failed, why aren't you going to fail? My students at FSU would never weep in class. They might say, "Fuck you, Levine," but never would they weep. Why so many wonderful poets from this funny little school in central California, all of whom came as local youngsters coming to college, not a single one recruited—Larry Levis, Lawson Inada, Gary Soto, Roberta Spear, David St. John, Luis Omar Salinas, Greg Pape, Glover Davis, Sherley Williams, Herb Scott, Kathy Fagan, Leonard Adame, Ernesto Trejo, Jon Veinberg, Robert Vasquez, and more I'm forgetting. It's not because of the teacher. We know how little a teacher can do. These poets could accept their failures as poets and as people, learn from them, and go on. And I didn't stop them by distracting them with long tedious lectures on how and why we should master the sestina. I didn't assign them hundred-line poems without adjectives on the theme of cuisine. I did not tell them what words they had to rhyme on—*El Salvador* or *Aperitif,* depending on how trendy I was feeling.

Hemingway tells us that all of his early fiction was lost; it was in a trunk that his wife somehow mislabeled or missent, and it vanished. He might have been lying. He couldn't lie all the time, so he might have for once been telling the truth. In any case, he says it was the most fortunate thing that ever happened to him as a young writer. It makes a good yarn. The significant thing is that he didn't try to recreate the lost work; he went on from where he was. I had a similar thing happen to me; I had all my early poems swiped. They were in a suitcase that was stolen out of the trunk of my car. I'm sure the thief was enormously disappointed he didn't get the poems of Wallace Stevens. It happened in Detroit, which is a corrupt city, so I was able to get them back. I was incredibly anxious before the deal was completed and the poems were once again my own. I can remember reading them in the light of this escapade and realizing that while I was happy to have them back it would have been no big deal if I'd never reclaimed them. There wasn't that much there. I had no laurels to rest on; my poetry was in the future or nowhere. A lesson worth learning. At the same time, 1953, I was writing those swiped and returned poems, I had a friend writing poems that he later published in his first book, which appeared in 1961. A second edition came out in 1967, and he had revised those already heavily revised poems. He was now a middle-aged man toiling over the poems of his twenties. He has gone on to do nothing of interest. How he could have used my thief.

I had one great teacher of poetry writing, John Berryman, and I believe one is enough. He was my teacher for a single semester, and I believe a single semester is plenty. I got two wonderful pieces of advice from him. The first: When young, write everything that occurs to you to write. The other was a lesson by example: when we parted he said, "Sometime in the future, a year or so from now, send me four or five poems, and I'll write and tell you how I think you're doing." I waited a year and a half, sent him some poems, and he wrote back carefully assessing my progress and lack of same. And that was it; it was over. I never wanted or needed another teacher. I was his student for fifteen weeks; I either had some brains and got what he had to say or I was hopeless and didn't get it. Don't make a career of being a student. Try it a few times and become a poet or don't.

In conclusion, I would like to answer a question that was asked the other day. Someone in the audience asked the panel to deal with the aspects of one's writing that are either political or spiritual—that is, when one gets to the place where the two roads diverge, which road do you take, the one marked "political" or the other, "spiritual." My answer is quite simple: We live in a time in which the spiritual is political. I am vividly aware that the government that rules this land is trying to crush my spirit, to crush the spirits of all of us, so that we will soddenly, weakly, tiredly, do as we are told. I think that any poem or novel or story or play that demonstrates the beauty and unkillable toughness of the human spirit is a political act that inspires us to be what we can be, independent people. There is no conflict between being political and being spiritual.

Neruda y Yo

Back in the late 1940s when I was a young poetry maniac attending Wayne University in Detroit with other young poetry maniacs, most of us seemed to be of two minds, and I— for better or worse—was of three. How I envied the most popular teachers of English, those tall, willowy assistant professors from Eastern universities; they were the masters of the complexity of the obvious, experts of paradox and irony, total wizards in the face of any text. They taught Milton, John Donne, George Herbert, and, of course, the god of the hour, T. S. Eliot. (When Dylan Thomas entered the arena, they skulked in the shadows and pretended nothing was happening.) Never once did I visit one of their offices without having to wait first for at least forty minutes while behind closed doors they counseled the best-looking and most neurotic young women, who would issue forth in a cloud of their own tobacco smoke looking as though they had at last encountered sanity and wisdom. Needless to say, I went unnoticed. These young men did not write poetry, or if they did they did so in secret. They did not say that all the worthy poetry had been written; that would have been too obvious to say. I envied them not only the neurotic young heartbreaking women, but what seemed to me to be what summoned those women, a sense of mastery and control, what Spaniards call "the habit of command," something I lacked totally, what with my emotions spilling over on everything.

I was trying to write poetry; that was my second mind. After reading Sherwood Anderson and John Dos Passos, it

From *Manoa* 3, no. 1, "Neruda y Yo," 1991.

struck me like thunder that nothing like this existed in our poetry, nothing that included the actual world with its Professors of Sanity, its neurotic lovely women, and the inarticulate, frustrated poet I had become. Where else could I go to master my chosen "craft and sullen art" if not to the university, and yet it was a place that seemed to take not the slightest interest in my quest for a relevant, a "Detroit" (if you will), poetry? Out of this and out of who knows how many slights and failures came my third mind: a desire for instant revenge and redemption, a spiritual recklessness and love of recklessness, a total fury toward what I knew of academia for its snobbery and unearned sense of self-satisfaction. All of what I hated about Wayne was most perfectly typified by one class I had in Nineteenth-Century American Literature, which took place in a building at the busy corner of West Warren and Second Avenue. Every time the light at Warren went from red to green the huge semis would crank up and race toward Third, beyond which was US 24 and the larger world; of course, they completely drowned out the voice of our teacher, who went right on lecturing as though he were ensconced within the original ivory tower. For me, dear Professor Princeton was academia, and when he said that Emily Dickinson burned "with a hard gemlike flame," I wanted to drag him off screaming to the foundry at Ford Rouge so he could see for the first time in his life a hard gemlike flame. Why we so docilely endured him I don't know. Clearly, we should have at least cast him in bronze so he could have been publicly the monument he already privately was.

Then Pablo Neruda entered my life. My week was built around attending classes, meeting with my fellow poets Thursday afternoons at the Miles Poetry Room in the Wayne Library, and working just enough to survive and dress with enough élan to facilitate my pursuit of beauty and love. That is where Neruda entered, as my comrade in the pursuit of sex and my co-conspirator in the destruction of the Institutions of Sanity and Higher Learning. On an afternoon in early October 1948 in the Miles Room we met over his poem "Widower's Tango":

I have gone back to single bedrooms,
to cold lunches in restaurants, and I
drop my pants and my shirts on the floor as I used to.

Here he was, a famous poet in middle age, a Chilean who had never ventured near Detroit, and he knew or imagined my existence better than I knew it. Moreover, he knew that it was through my own mastery of the tango, the fox-trot, and the rumba that I pursued my solitary search for beauty in the great dance halls on Woodward Avenue. He knew what I did not, the intensity and meaning of my own yearnings, which were a secret to everyone including me, for if challenged I would have told myself the old lie, I'm just chasing pussy. Mysteriously, he knew how unknowable and profound was my need:

And to hear you make water, in the darkness, at the
    bottom of the house,
as though you were pouring a slow, tremulous, silvery,
    obstinate honey,
how many times over would I yield up this choir of
    shadows which I possess,
and the clash of useless swords which is audible in my soul,
and the dove of blood, alone on my forehead,
calling to things which have vanished, to beings who
    have vanished,
to substances incomprehensibly inseparable and lost.

Here too was the companion of my third mind, the one I needed most and knew the least about, for at twenty I could be seized by an overpowering anger toward all creation, a loathing for the million pieces of ugliness in which I seemed to be drowning alone. Suddenly there was a companionable voice blowing softly in my ear, the words redolent of milk, brandy, sea air, even in the English versions of Angel Flores, now long out of print and stolen from my library. It was like finding a piece of myself where I least expected to find it, in the library:

> I do not want to go on being a root in the dark,
> hesitating, stretched out, shivering with dreams,
> downwards, in the wet tripe of the earth,
> soaking it up and thinking, eating every day.

The more I read the more I discovered myself in this curious wanderer of the cities, this poet with his inexhaustible need to see, touch, smell, hear, all that was around and within him. He took his hat in his hand, closed the door behind him, and went in search of our lives, turning away from nothing.

> I stride along with calm, with eyes, with shoes,
> with fury, with forgetfulness,
> I pass, I cross offices and stores full of orthopedic
>   appliances,
> and courtyards hung with clothes hanging from a wire.

Daily I too would pass the office buildings and stores where I had worked, the grim shops where I had failed to sell that set of wrenches or a dozen hand-colored photo enlargements or a genuine gold-plated ID bracelet. There where the little defeats were still tallied and sorted, I would pass and say to myself in the words of my new mentor and companion,

> it would be delicious
> to scare a notary with a cut lily
> or knock a nun stone dead with one blow of an ear.
> It would be beautiful
> to go through the streets with a green knife
> shouting until I died of cold.

Here was a body of poetry to join the other art that nourished my heart and had little or no place in academia—jazz. Like the jazz I was hearing in Detroit, bebop, Neruda captured the chaotic quality of our everyday lives, the rhythms of the streets, the cadences of our speech, the very swing of our walks. Jazz was being created all around me, by my own classmates, the great Boppers to be, Kenny Burrell, Tommy Flannagan, Bess Bonnier, Pepper Adams. If I could give back to Detroit a poetry as worthy as the music these young people were creating, I knew I would be the Neruda of Michigan. As he had redefined Chile as "the sweet waist of America," I might bring a new name and nature to Detroit. Forty years later I'm still trying.

ello

It would be wrong to end this without two afterthoughts, one regarding the poetry of Neruda, one not.

First the not: the Wayne English Department was a more interesting and various group than this sketch suggests. There were some truly inspiring old-timers. I shall never forget our master of Shakespeare hauling his young Eastern office partner into the hall outside their office and telling him calmy and sanely that if ever again he heard the spoiled pup talking to a student as though he were a piece of shit he'd throw him down the stairs. "To you," he said, "that kid is just a dumb Polack, but you took a job to teach him how to write. Now get back in there and teach him or get off this campus." That kid was not me, but he could have been, and I knew Leo Kirschbaum was defending my right to an education. The Neruda note: During the Vietnam War I was part of a large protest group in Fresno called The Resistance; as such and as a poet, I was invited up to the East Bay to give a speech and a short poetry reading as part of a gigantic antiwar march that would take place the next day in San Francisco. The venue for my performance was an almost deserted high school football stadium. By the time I got up to talk, the fog settling gloomily over the place, I had heard perhaps a dozen earnest young people tell the freezing audience how on the next day we were going to stop the war. This was, I supposed, at best a fantasy, at worst an inspiring lie. I said what I truly believed: tomorrow we will march and not stop the war. I was booed, which did not surprise me. I responded that the fight for liberty and justice never ended, for the enemies of our freedom were always with us and were always more powerful than we, and I turned to Pablo Neruda's great poem "Letter to Miguel Otero Silva in Caracas," which tells of a failing labor strike on the nitrate flats in Tarapaca and how Neruda felt the loss coming and with it his old sense of depression and self-hate returning. In that moment when they could have been beaten a little pale girl recited a poem of Otero Silva, an old poem "that wanders among the wrinkled eyes / of all the workers of my country, of America. / And that small piece of your poetry blazed suddenly." And they took heart again. But before the poem ends Neruda reminds us that there are always the tortured among us, "the jails where people disappeared forever," and at the very moment he writes his poem "a rotten leader / has put the best men of my country under the earth." That is why Otero Silva writes his songs, "so that someday the disgraced and wounded America" can gather its gifts "without the terrifying blood of beatings, coagulated / on the hands of the executioners and the businessmen." When I finished his poem, I felt a calm flow into me and those around me. Win or lose, I knew many of us would go on with the struggle for decency.

Two Journeys

Is what follows a fiction by Balzac? It would seem unlikely, for there is no one standing out in the dark on a rain-swept night as a carriage pulled by six gray horses splashes down the Boulevard Raspail on the way to the apartment of that singularly beautiful woman, Madame La Pointe, although it does involve a beautiful and singularly gifted woman. Is it a fiction at all? That is a harder question to deal with. If Norman Mailer had written it and its central character was a novelist living in Brooklyn, the author of an astonishingly successful first book called *The Naked and the Dead,* a man deeply immersed in an ongoing depiction of the CIA, he would describe it as a fiction, and he would most likely name the central character Norman Mailer. One of my central characters is named Philip Levine; he is a poet from Detroit, he lives mainly in Fresno, California, where he has an awful job teaching too many courses in freshman comp at the local college, and on this particular summer day he is traveling by train with two fellow poets to give a reading almost no one will attend. It is twenty years ago, he is in his fiftieth year, as I was then, and, though I cannot call it a fiction, I will begin now to fictionalize this tale.

I will say the local railway has a reputation for first-rate service; they are never more than a few minutes late even in the worst weather, and on this day the weather is a delight: blue sky with a few puffy clouds overhead as the poets head for the provincial town where their reading, though almost entirely unadvertised, will become the event of that summer's cultural history, a history that will never be written except for the present effort, which since it may be a fiction may not be a history at

From the *Michigan Quarterly Review,* "Two Journeys," (summer 1997).

all. Shall I say that the events I am about to recount are as true as an old man's memory allows them to be? No, that would not be true, for I am about to give the other two poets fictional names and disguise them so as to protect them. Protect them from what or from whom? Neither does anything to be ashamed of; indeed both behave with marvelous integrity. I will protect them from me, that untrustworthy poet who might alchemize them into former production line workers or assemblers of universal joints and thus ennoble them to a degree that would appall both them and you. I will remain Philip Levine, forty-nine years old, six months from my seventh book of poetry, *The Names of the Lost,* and my first terrible reviews by that great friend to poetry, the *New York Times.* The man, just approaching middle age, is slender, taller than I, and though still in his thirties his hair is beginning to go gray, but he is far more youthful and youthful looking than I, and unlike me he dresses with good taste. His name, Gabriel Sienna. The woman is even younger; she is fair-haired, delicately constructed, and in the soft light falling into our car very beautiful—I shall call her Elaine Langer; though she cannot be much over thirty, her poems have already begun to attract enormous attention. I am pleased to be here with these two, who I am beginning to like far more than I expected. Sienna, I had heard, was something of a dandy and a political conservative, but for the past several days I have observed him treating working-class people—waiters, maids, cab drivers, cops, train conductors—with a grace and regard that I immediately recognized was part of his democratic nature. Elaine had been a mystery to me. I had met her only twice before, when we'd read together in New York City and Iowa, and both times she had insisted on referring to me as the star. To me a star was Marlon Brando or Willie Mays, so I had assumed— incorrectly—that she was either ditzy or sucking up to me in the hopes I might advance her career, but it was now clear to me that she was not so stupid as to think I was endowed to advance anyone's career, even my own. In the few days we'd been traveling together it had become clear that she was neither ditzy nor a careerist: she was simply a shy woman. That she had not the least interest in me or Sienna as sexual or romantic beings was clear from the moment we'd assembled in the capital, for she was mad about another man, a very handsome, stylishly dressed young man who sat sleeping across the aisle from the three of us, perhaps exhausted by the previous night.

To our mutual delight Sienna and I had discovered that before this trip we had both been rereading *The Prelude* by Wordsworth and finding it both awesome and inspiring. For me this was largely unexpected, for I had not read the entire poem since my undergraduate days, when my professor had forced a class of a dozen students to race through it in less than a week and to keep our eyes open for the key passages that might indicate its deeper themes. Rereading the poem in my own sweet time I discovered the majesty of passage after passage, which reaffirmed my belief in this art I seemed to be giving my life to. Elaine broke in at one point to express her astonishment that two active poets would spend so much of their summers on so dated a text and would both feel the experience had fueled their own work. She was not in the least critical. To the contrary; she was utterly charmed and vowed that when these readings were over and she was home she would sit down with Wordsworth and Keats (who had been the topic of the previous day's train conversation) and discover for herself these treasures. Here the fiction or the history or the poem—for as Edwin Muir has reminded us, "the poet's first allegiance is to imaginative truth" and "if he is to serve mankind that is the only way he can do it"—grows crucial, for one of us, Sienna or I, asks where she had received her education in poetry. (For the purposes of this "history" I will invent a university and place it in Peoria, the University of Ambition, famous for its dedication to the arts, often referred to as "the Athens of Central Illinois.") Elaine answers, "U of A," and Sienna then inquires if she had not been obliged to read the great Romantics. At this point tears well up in her eyes, and it is clear that some memory just come upon her is devastatingly painful. The three of us are silent for several minutes.

Elaine wipes her eyes with the back of her hand; she does not cry. She begins a slow explanation: she had gone to the university with the express purpose of becoming a poet. She was some years older than the other entering students having done "other things" after finishing high school, and one of the other things was to try to become a writer on her own, chiefly a writer of poetry. She knew no one in her New Jersey town who wrote poetry so she had to go it alone and discover what she could. In the local library and in New York City bookstores she happened upon three kindred spirits: Louise Bogan, James Wright, and Theodore Roethke, but she was sure there were many others and hence her enrollment at U of A. Her entrance scores were good enough to allow her into poetry writing and a "period course" in the Romantic poets, courses usually reserved for juniors and seniors. "So you've read Keats and Wordsworth," I say, "and you've been sitting here for two days listening to us mis-describe their great poems." Once again I had it wrong. While they were still on Blake and what her teacher termed "the Pre-Romantic poets," he had asked her to visit his office so that they might discuss her Blake paper. And then she laughs, her face full of lively animation as well as sorrow. They never got to her paper. Tweedy Professor X put down his unlighted pipe and launched into a spiel about the evils of nursing an unacted desire, both his and hers, for he was quite sure they felt *that way* about each other. The lust of the goat, he assured her, is the bounty of God, and one law for the lion and ox is oppression (he didn't say which one he was); he placed a long-fingered hairless hand on her knee. "Long fingered and hairless," she repeats, "I will remember that hand for as long as I live." She felt the sweat leap from her pores, and for a moment she thought she would faint. "What did you do?" asks Sienna. "I just got out of there." She dropped the course.

Elaine goes on to explain that it was actually more serious than it sounded in the telling, for she began for the first time in her life to doubt the value of poetry, to doubt the whole enterprise. This of course was noticed by her poetry writing instructor, a short, balding man much impressed with his own wit and vitality. He required the students to turn in poems written according to strict formal demands. He had lavishly praised her first two attempts, ten heroic couplets and a Petrarchan sonnet, which were followed by no villanelle, no pantoum, no narrative in blank verse. Professor Y, or Mac, as he insisted his students call him, asked Elaine to stay after class on their sixth meeting. When the other students had departed, he closed the classroom door, turned suddenly toward her, and literally shouted, "What the fuck is going on?" He began a long rap on the theme of her special gifts and his generosity in allowing her into the class in the first place. Before she could begin to describe her own problem, he launched into a tirade on the need for these beginners to follow the proper path, the path their elders had followed, the path that had produced such giants as Nemerov and Justice. She tried to assure him that her situation had nothing to do with the ongoing quarrels over formalism and free verse. "You have the talent to become a published poet within a year, and I have the clout to see you are published. I've done it for others." And then he began to rattle off the poets he'd "made," a word he used before each woman's name. His hands were short and plump; they looked as though they'd never picked up anything heavier than a check, and he placed one on her shoulder and began to slide it down toward her left breast when she rose and called him a "fat pig." She dropped out of the university that afternoon. "I'd had such hopes for the place," she says and goes on to describe her bus ride to Chicago, her confusing hours there, wondering if she'd done the right thing, and then the even longer lonely trip back to New Jersey. She spent the year as an office worker for a textbook publisher in New York City commuting from her parents' place.

"When did you get back to poetry?" Sienna asks. Within a month or so she realized she could not let herself be scarred by those two creeps; poetry was something she had to write, if only for herself. "It's a long story," she says, "but I had the good fortune to discover through a course at the 92nd Street Y a true mentor, also a man, but one who cared about me as a person as well as my work." Her lover, Daniel, has wakened across the aisle and is stretching himself. The train is drawing through the green suburbs of our destination; we pass tennis courts, most of them in use, a small white church, and then enter a darkened tunnel only to emerge into the terminal. We rise, and that conversation comes to an end forever as Daniel struggles with the two huge suitcases loaded with the clothes, makeup, and *chatchkes* of this small and determined woman.

Is the fiction you've just read true? If Aristotle in the *Poetics* is right, then it is truer than history, or, to quote Edwin Muir again, it is "a symbolic stage on which the drama of human life can play itself out." Let me ask a more essential question: Is it of any use? Does it contain any nuggets of wisdom you can take with you on the long voyage toward a life in poetry or, if you would prefer, a life without poetry? Poetry itself we know is of use. How do we know such a thing, stated so finally by me as a fact that might sit beside such assertions as "all men are mortal" or "Michael Jordan wears Nikes"? I could answer as Keats would have, that I have tested it on my pulse and felt that pulse surge—a fact—and I knew that I was alive to a degree rare in my experience. Or as the contemporary poet Jane Cooper has written, "Poetry can be *useful* in providing us with a theater of total human responses." Cooper was in the process of defining the essential qualities of that very essential poet Muriel Rukeyser, who herself wrote in her book *The Life of Poetry*, "The making of a poem is the type of act which releases aggression. Since it is released appropriately, it is creation." If your nature is totally pragmatic you might demand to know if Marvell's "To His Coy Mistress," when heard by his beloved—for surely he intoned it to her in his rich baritone— caused her to become so much less coy that she rewarded his advances. A question I, of course, can't answer, but if Rukeyser is right, and I believe she is, it hardly matters, for the poem itself was an act of creation the rest of us have had to joy in for centuries. If that other act of creation never transpired, it may have mattered enormously to Andrew Marvell or perhaps not at all, for the poem may merely have been that symbolic stage Muir referred to.

Before I get back to the three poets in the provincial terminal waiting impatiently on wooden benches for the promised host to collect them—and Daniel, the lover, as well—and escort them to their hotel and there complete arrangements for that night's dinner and reading, I have something of a parable to share with you, one that deals with a life with poetry and a life without poetry. At age eighteen, when I found the poetry in English of the last century and a half—Stephen Crane first, then Eliot, Auden, Spender, Wilfred Owen, Dylan Thomas, Yeats, Hardy, Stevens, Frost, Dickinson, Whitman, and finally Williams—I thought that without these words life would be a pale thing. I took Williams's famous words from "Asphodel, that Greeny Flower" very seriously and recited them to any innocent victim I could corner:

> It is difficult
> to get the news from poems
> yet men die miserably every day
> for lack
> of what is found there.

I took them to be about me and everyone else. To the credit of my patient students, many of whom went on to become poets while others opted for careers in law, medicine, wine making, journalism, organic farming, housewifery, and the military, when I stated and restated the absolute need of poetry in every life, no one laughed in my face or contradicted me.

Fortunately not everyone was so docile. At a poetry conference in Bisbee, Arizona, about a dozen years ago I went into my usual rant about the essential need for poetry in each life. No one in the audience blinked, but on the panel with me was that wonderful and very wise poet Robert Duncan, who after hearing me out gently corrected me. He reminded me that we are not all alike: what turns some of us on bores others to death. He asked me if that indeed had not been my experience. Indeed it had been, I agreed, for at one time I had hoped that all productions of Wagner's operas be staged underwater, music that Mark Twain had once remarked was not as bad as it sounded. From then on I stopped badgering my students and friends and any other captive audiences. After listening to Duncan I came to believe that the teacher's function was not to force an art down the throats of his students but rather to help them find the art that thrilled their hearts.

Now for the parable. It bears some resemblance to the "history" or fiction of the three poets journeying to their reading, though there is one difference: it is composed of nothing but facts. It involves a poet journeying to a reading, a lone poet, one of the very same three, Levine, now a bit older, a bit tougher having survived a number of bad reviews, but not so tough that passing over the island of Manhattan, where he will spend the weekend with his oldest son and then read for a small mob at the 92nd Street Y, he does not feel his secret heart swell with excitement, his pulse quicken, his breath surge as though he had just heard Galway Kinnell recite one of those magical passages from his great poem "The Avenue Bearing the Initial of Christ into the New World." So excited and perhaps foolish is he at that moment that he turns to the man seated next to him and says something profound, like "Isn't that amazing!" The man, a large, besuited fellow who has had his head stuck in a huge tome depicting some of the world's longest bridges, leans across Levine's lap to have a look and says, "My." A conversation ensues. The large man, it turns out, is headed for a conference on the uses of reinforced concrete. It will convene on Monday, at noon, in a large hotel that is part of the complex known as Dulles Airport. He had planned to change planes at La Guardia and fly directly to Dulles, although this is Saturday afternoon, and he could just as easily spend two nights in New York City, for he is on an expense account. Levine calms the fellow's fears regarding the dangers of the city and assures him that if he stays away from the wrong neighborhoods he'll be just as safe as he'd be in Indianapolis, where he works and lives. What could he do in New York? he wonders aloud. Almost anything, Levine replies. What are you interested in? No response. Does he like painting? The museums are among the best in the world. Painting is okay. How about theater or movies? A tepid response. Levine tries food, for every sort of ethnic food is available. Well, the fellow has to watch his weight, and he jabs a thick forefinger into his barely pouching waist and goes on to describe his incredible exercise regimen, though he avoids lifting weights for that can give you a false sense of power. Levine runs through dance, jazz, classical music, rock— which it turns out gives the fellow terrible headaches; just walking the streets of what is probably the world's most energetic city can be a heady experience. The cement maven sits impassively. Levine offers to share a cab in from La Guardia and direct him to a nice hotel. After a long silence the poet says, I think it's probably best if you get to Dulles as quickly as possible.

So while I believe Duncan was right and since receiving his tactful remarks on my position regarding the situation of poetry in the world, I have never again browbeaten those who do not respond to it, write it, care if it exists at all. I have come to believe that something must be there to, as Jane Cooper so aptly put it, "provide us with a theater of total human responses." My seatmate on that flight into La Guardia is the perfect example of someone who lacks that theater, who seems to have no idea such a thing could exist. An educated man with a degree in engineering from Purdue, he must once or twice in his life have attended to a poem and barely noticed it as it flew by him on its way to glory. In my description of our conversation I left out one detail that occurred near its end: out of some growing distaste for the man as well as to determine the degree to which he had stopped being a total person, I added that Manhattan was full of the sexiest people I had ever seen, both men and women, and their styles of walking, talking, dress, made it clear just what treasures they possessed. For all he seemed to care I might have been describing varieties of apples. I went on: "You just see them on the streets in Midtown or in the Village or Soho at all hours, bodies and faces the likes of which never filled the streets of the Midwest." His only response was, "I am married," which suggested to me not his moral rectitude—which may have been wonderfully intact—but his total lack of curiosity as to how people have been behaving for the last few thousand years.

I have at times considered a world totally without music and reacted with a horror so absolute that I immediately knew it was the art that fired my heart and blood like no other even though I have no talent for it. Thanks to the discoveries of Thomas Edison I have it even without New York City. Indeed in Fresno, where I have lived longer than anywhere else, I have it each morning when I waken to the mockingbirds doing their thing from on high in the Atlas cedar that grows in my front yard. But the art I have pursued for better or worse for over fifty years is poetry, and I have found it an enterprise worthy of a human life, and I haven't the least notion if anything I have written will in the hearts of others outlive me. Why, you might well ask, with that knowledge do I call it an enterprise worthy of a human life? Because I have been part of something far larger than myself: I have been part of the attempt to verbalize as precisely as possible what it has meant to live through the great depression, the horrors of World War II, the fiasco of anticommunism, the long, painful failed struggle for racial justice, and wind up in old age in a country gone to ruin through the greed of capitalism with a technology that can take us to the moon while our streets are stained by the lives of the poor and the homeless, the present world of Microsoft, unfettered pollution, the epidemic of murderous drugs, and the economic policies of Ronald Reagan. I have been part of the generation of Adrienne Rich, John Ashbery, Galway Kinnell, W. S. Merwin, Robert Creeley, Anthony Hecht, Denise Levertov, Etheridge Knight, Sylvia Plath, Allen Ginsberg, Gary Snyder: we have done our best to capture the century in verse. We have told America, and the rest of the world should it care to listen, what it's been like living through this age. We have been useful.

What has become of the three poets just arrived in the provincial town of X, justly famous for its cathedral and its filthy brown river that drags slowly through the town? With Daniel the two men grow restless and begin to pace the gradually emptying train station while Elaine sits composedly staring off into the dusty building at nothing in particular. At last the emissary arrives with two taxis in tow, thank heavens for no single taxi can handle all the luggage Elaine has loaded upon the shoulders of her young lover as well as the three poets and their host. She, the emissary, is breathless and apologetic, and her apologies are quickly accepted, for the poets have learned they in fact have hotel rooms, plans for dinner, and an almost totally unannounced reading to give that night. The emissary, Catherine, who prefers to be called Cate, is both a younger and more attractive woman than those usually strapped with these functions; today she seems flustered and more than a little overwhelmed by her duties. Even before we reach the hotel we are warned that it is not top-notch as the local arts council is strapped for cash and also that due to a screwup by some hireling of the council the only advertising

for the event consists of small posters placed "in just the important places" that very Saturday morning by Cate herself. "To
have great poetry you need great audiences," Whitman had
written, but I learned that night what I had suspected for
years, that for once at least good father Walt was wrong.

After being deposited in our mediocre digs—one room
with two single beds for Sienna and me, bath down the hall—
we are free for some hours to walk the almost deserted town,
inspect the massive local cathedral, and gaze longingly into
the sluggish river a dozen local boys find suitable for a dip. We
return to our room in time to shower and dress in the expected jackets and ties and meet with Elaine and Daniel in the
tiny chairless lobby, where a waiting Cate leads us a few blocks
to a modest restaurant. The meal begins with something I still
believe the waitress called sorghum soup and goes rapidly
downhill from there. Cate keeps reminding us not to expect a
crowd. No, there will be no books available for signing and
sale; no one at the arts council knew how to go about obtain-
ing them. When we arrive on foot at the community house at
which we will read there is no audience at all besides the three
young men arranging the lights and moving some of the furniture out of the way, for in fact we will be reading on the set of a
Pinter play that will have its first performance the following
week. We wait in silence until fifteen minutes past the assigned
hour, but no one arrives. I ask the lighting technicians to stay
and along with Cate to become our audience, and two agree to
do so; the third has made arrangments for the evening but
promises to return as soon as possible with his girlfriend. I
read first after introducing myself, for Cate has confessed she
has no idea who we are, what we have published if anything,
and what our work might be about. I read as well as I have
ever read, finding unusual strength in my voice and aiming
my words toward my two fellow poets who have heard me for
several nights in a row but never before seemed so alert to
what I was reading. Elaine reads next after a short introduction by me; it is by far the best reading I have ever heard her
give. She is usually nervous to the point of being almost inaud-
ible, directing her attention not to her listeners but rather to
an invisible audience riding ten or twelve feet above the actual

one, but this night she looks directly into my eyes. I hear the fullness of her language, the delicacy of her rhythms, and the startling freshness of her tropes as I've never heard them before. She introduces the poems with only their titles and launches them into the utter silence of the room in a strong alto voice. Sienna comes next. He begins with no wisecracks or small talk but instead goes into a long and extraordinarily moving elegy to his father, which he follows with three short lyric poems; this is far more daring and powerful work than he is known for. When he finishes the six of us—Elaine, Daniel, Cate, the two technicians, and me—rise and applaud this stunning presentation and its creator. Before we can leave for drinks at the local watering hole "on the arts council," the third technician returns with his stunningly attractive friend in tow, and they are assured they have missed something astonishing. I suggest that each of us poets read one poem for these two, and to my surprise my fellow poets are equally enthusiastic. The magic is still there.

What startled me most and what I recall most clearly from that night was my sudden and overwhelming discovery of Elaine's poetry. For the first time I was truly getting it. Even in the theater of my mind, alone with the poem on the page, I had not attended to it with the intensity and passion it demanded. I had been reading her work as a series of bright moves, of smart decisions, I had been hearing harmonious phrases and lines moving gracefully from one to another, careful pacing and lovely ploys that brought the poems to a satisfying closure. That night I heard a unique human voice calling out from the deepest roots of its nature, calling out to be heard by what was deepest and most human in me. I was hearing poetry. We here in America have been practicing this art for hundreds of years almost without an audience for the single reason that we must in exactly the way a born dancer must respond to the music. That night Elaine had an audience—I know that as well as I know anything—and though it may have been only an audience of one, the act was complete, for one human being had reached across the immense gulf our education has taught us exists between each of us, had reached across that gulf through the magic of her language to remind me I was human.

Let me return to a question I asked earlier as a way of avoiding the question of the truth of this narrative: what use is this story? I think it contains two extraordinary truths about a life in poetry. The first is that we as poets (and no doubt also as people) need each other. As a boy first composing poetry at age thirteen I truly believed that some day I would be addressing the world. I was perfectly able to wait for that day, for the composing itself was such a delicious experience. Even at eighteen when I began my second career as a poet—my first was quite short, lasting less than three years and fortunately producing nothing that is extant—I thought that what I wrote in both prose and verse would have an enormous influence on the way my fellow citizens behaved toward themselves and each other. I had every reason to believe this, for the writers I was reading, especially the fiction writers (Dreiser, Dos Passos, Chekhov, Dostoyevsky, Balzac, Sherwood Anderson) were creating a me I had not known could exist. Within a year I would read Keats's letters, for me the most extraordinary document on what it means to be a poet, and again become someone else. Through the agency of his letter to his brother George on the world as the *Vale of Soul Making* I felt myself becoming a religious person. In the letter he asks George, and because the letter has been preserved those of us who will follow, what the use of a world like ours is and goes on to define that use. "There may be intelligences or sparks of divinity in millions," he writes, "but they are not Souls till they acquire identities, till each one is personally itself." And how will this happen? "How, but by the medium of a world like this?" In order to clarify what he only dimly perceives he puts it "in the most homely form possible," and he goes on to tell George and us that the world is the horn book from which each intelligence learns to read, that is, to become what it is capable of becoming, a singular identity, a soul; without the education our experience of *this* world can give us we remain less than a soul, merely a potential. It is an extraordinary vision for a twenty-three-year-old man to coin to account for human suffering, which Keats knew full well as an apprentice surgeon working in a London hospital, but then Keats was one of the most extraordinary twenty-three-year-olds who ever lived. As the oldest of four siblings and with both parents long dead, Keats was deprived of what most of us take for granted, an adolescence. He had to become a man at a very early age; he had even to nurse his younger brother Tom through the final stages of TB to his death at eighteen. When he asked after the use of a world like ours he knew that world in its glory—his poems attest to that—and in its savagery. If Keats is right, the experience of this world can school each one of us into becoming a soul, and of course literature is part of the experience the world gives us. That night of the reading with an audience of no more than eight and no less than one, Elaine revived a human soul.

A genius such as Rimbaud or Dickinson or Blake can go it alone. There are those among us who are so gifted and so furiously and originally motivated that nothing can stop them from becoming poets except themselves. The rest of us need each other; we need to know this largely ignored art is still cherished and useful to others, and we need each other's counsel and encouragement to stay the course. (I suspect many of you have learned this or you wouldn't be at a place like this.) In my thirty-something years of teaching I've seen it over and over: one truly gifted and generous aspiring poet can excite an entire class and direct them to a poetry they did not know they possessed. In the fall of 1961 a psychology major trying his hand at writing in my first poetry writing class rose in the back of the room and asked if he might offer a poem to the class. Thinking no harm could come from this I let him recite a piece he had not yet written down. It began thusly:

If a broken-down roan in a fenced-in field had only two
    legs would it be a man?
If a spotted dog wearing a napkin had one leg would it be
    a Republican?
If a man had common sense would the governor make
    him pick clover for the next two thousand years?
In my last incarnation I looked for the perfect apple and
    so walked from Albany to Sacramento
And chain-smoked the entire way.
My health is better for it so don't believe anything you
    read.

His name was Charles Moulton, and he was a genuine Fresno surrealist. To say the class never quite recovered from the experience is an understatement. Moulton had managed in a few minutes to fire the imaginations of twenty young and not so young poets who suddenly understood it was open house and that whatever the brain concocted was material for poetry. A few years later it was an entering freshman, Larry Levis, who wrote,

> He numbed himself to photographs
> of farmers swatting flames off their faces.
> He lived at least
> as well as a cold rat,
> waiting for his number to come up.

Yes, even the draft was material for poetry; Larry's classmates began to write utterly surprising poems that struggled with the agony and humor of coming to age or middle age in their brutal Central Valley towns. Two years later it was the lyricism of David St. John, also a freshman, that did the trick; later the sardonic anger of Sherley Williams and Gary Soto. It's amazing how far we can go with each other's help. I remember telling this to a young poet who believed he belonged to a rising tide of poets of social commitment. Once he discovered there was no such tide he felt betrayed by poetry. He truly believed poetry owed him fame, as though someone or something named poetry had asked for his help, his life. He cut himself off from his former friends and transformed himself into a minor mandarin and a footnote. He'd also accepted the myth that we must remain solitary and write out of the sources of our deepest wounding. I believe the truth is we form a family with other poets, living and dead, or we risk going nowhere.

The second truth I also learned from Elaine. The impulse, the drive, if you will, to write poetry is incredibly powerful. In spite of the worst efforts of two terrible men disguised as teachers, Elaine had only briefly been sidetracked. This young woman who at less than a hundred pounds and, as her early photographs attest, of a delicate beauty and, as I learned through the contact of some weeks, of a delicate emotional constitution, contained an unkillable need to create true poetry, to build that "theater of total human responses." Each of us no doubt takes a differing and private route to this art (or in some cases away from it); those of us who need it, who see it as essential to our spiritual survival, will overcome the discouragements of an indifferent society and a corrupted literary world. We will do this simply because we have to. Why is this true? I believe the need to write poetry (and I assume prose fiction) is exactly like the need as Plato defines it to love, that is, to possess the halved soul's complement, to be whole. The sense of completeness that writing at our best gives is comparable to nothing else in my experience, but that is no doubt because I have no gift for music and can draw nothing that resembles anything. I don't see poetry as chief among the arts nor writing as chief among human vocations. Rather I see imaginative writing as one among many useful pursuits. Not long ago I heard the great tenor saxophonist Sonny Rollins say of his life in music, "Everybody has something to do in this world." Being able to play the music he loves he found a blessing. Being able to play it with Gillespie, Hawkins, Max Roach, Clifford Brown, and Coltrane he found a blessing far beyond his early hopes. From what I know of Rollins's life—and I know a lot—like Elaine, nothing could stop him.

Of course when Rollins said each of us has something to do he meant something useful. In his case it was the making of music, and if you don't know why music is useful then there's nothing I can do to help you. And how useful is poetry? Let me go to one of the great writers of the century for a little help. In his essay "Why the Novel Matters" D. H. Lawrence writes, "As a man alive you may have a shot at your enemy. But as a ghastly simulacrum of life you may be firing bombs into men who are neither your friends or enemies, but things you are dead to: Which is criminal when the things happen to be alive." For Lawrence it is in the novel that we learn exactly what a man or woman alive is; by reading novels, "You can develop an instinct for life, if you will, instead of a theory of right and wrong, good and bad." The only three great novels Lawrence names in the essay are the Bible, Homer, and Shakespeare. He calls these "the supreme old novels," but, as any reader knows, two are poetry and the other when it is at its most eloquent is also poetry. I don't have to lecture you on how completely contemporary life can deaden us to what is alive; you have all experienced it enough for me not to add an ounce to your burden. "The grass withereth, the flower fadeth, but the Word of the Lord shall stand forever," quotes Lawrence and goes on to claim, "That's the kind of stuff we've drugged ourselves with," for the truth is the grass comes back, the flower dies and gives birth to new buds, but "the Word of the Lord, being man-uttered and a mere vibration on the ether, becomes staler and staler, more and more boring till at last we turn a deaf ear and it ceases to exist." But truly imaginative writing can bring us back to the living presence of the grass, to the fields that feed us, to the cities we live in and the nature of the men and women among whom we live.

> Tenderly will I use you curling grass,
> It may be you transpire from the breasts of young men,
> It may be if I had known them I would have loved them,
> It may be you are from old people, or from offspring
>   taken soon out of their mothers' laps,
> And here you are the mothers' laps.
>
> This grass is very dark to be from the white heads of old
>   mothers,
> Darker than the colorless beards of old men,
> Dark to come from under the faint red roofs of mouths.

In fact the greatest of our poets can make us come alive to the world in all its richness to a degree we scarcely believe.

I confess I not only find poetry useful these days, I find it absolutely necessary. I am presently living in one of the most complex, turbulent, disturbing, unfathomable communities in the world: New York City. Even my twenty-six years in industrial Detroit failed to prepare me for this. But through the work of its poets—Whitman, Hart Crane, García Lorca, and Galway Kinnell—I have come not only to a degree of peace with all the tumult; I have also become so comprehending of its presence that at times I can see its ordinary diurnal street life as the arena of the sublime and the sacred:

It is night, and raining. You look down
Toward Houston in the rain, the living streets,
Where instants of transcendence
Drift in oceans of loathing and fear, like lanternfishes,
Or phosphorous flashings in the sea, or the feverish light
Skin is said to give off when the swimmer drowns at night.

From the blind gut Pitt to the East River of Fishes
The Avenue cobbles a swath through the discolored air,
A roadway of refuse from the teeming shores and ghettos
And the Caribbean Paradise, into the new ghetto and new
    paradise,
This God-forsaken Avenue bearing the initial of Christ
Through the haste and carelessness of the ages,
The sea standing in heaps, which keeps on collapsing,
Where the drowned suffer a C-change,
And remain the common poor.

Through the magic of language I live my daily life in Kinnell's
City of God without God; that's how useful poetry can be.

What became of our three poets after their triumphant,
scarcely attended reading? Their host, Cate, walked them to
the local pub and there stood them to a drink on the arts
council, and then they stood her to one on their meager sti-
pends. The place was noisy with Saturday night celebrants,
and so the poetry party came to a rather abrupt ending. The
poets went off on foot to their shabby digs, at least two of them
with the intention of sleeping. Elaine and Daniel may have
had more serious work to do, for as Rilke reminds us those
who make love do a very essential work. Exhausted, Sienna
seemed to fall off before his head hit the pillow. Levine was
too wired from the reading, and for more than an hour he sat
on his bed writing in his journal that day's events without
knowing that some day, perhaps today, he would find them
useful. Finally he too grew weary and turned out the light and
welcomed the darkness. Perhaps he slept. In any case all three
poets rose the next morning from soiled beds to hurry off by
cab to the station for still another voyage to still another tiny
audience.

Let me close with a final cautionary tale. Some years ago I

received a letter from a very dear man who also wrote poetry, had in fact published several books though none recently and altogether only a fragment of what he had written. To put it bluntly he was and is what the world might call "a failed poet" though he is a gifted writer. He is both unlucky and without any clout in what I will call the "church temporal" of poetry, that world of ass-kissing and favor trading that brings so much useless work to acclaim. He had decided that even without a publisher he would put together his complete poems, and he did so under covers supplied by Kinko's. His letter was a response to this event, a dignified and touching letter that described his own emotions as he beheld this utterly unique volume. But he used one phrase that by now even he would regard as suspect; he wrote "now the granary is full." He sat for some weeks with this volume finding its presence less and less satisfying and finally sent it off to a university press. Knowing the speed with which any press deals with poetry he grew restless and uncharacteristically crabby. He told me later he put his household into a state of anxiety it had not known for over thirty years, since the coming of children. The cure for these ills was his own and obvious: his need to be a useful person could not be quieted, so complete poems or not he went back to the day to day undramatic work of trying to make poems. The truth is, poets need poetry as much as poetry needs poets. This man knew, as all of us who write poetry know, that if the work is worthy eventually it will find its readers. It may take more years than we have, as it did in the case of Dickinson and Kit Smart, but our job is the work of creation and as such it never ends.

I'm frequently asked, especially by students, how I got into poetry and what kept me going. I always tell the truth: once when I was very young I heard a knock at the door; I was home alone, and so I answered. There was a man in a bowler hat who asked if Philip Levine were home. "Yes," I said, "I am he." (Even then I was a stickler for grammar.) "My name is Tom Eliot," he said, "though you may know me as T. S. Eliot. I've come to tell you that American poetry needs you." What he was doing in a lower-middle-class neighborhood in Detroit, a Jewish neighborhood no less, I wasn't sure, but as our only Poet Nobelist could I refuse him? You don't believe that and you shouldn't. No one asked me to try to become a poet; it's what I chose to do, and it's what I choose to continue to do, and if it takes me nowhere I have no one to thank except myself.

II. Conversations and Interviews

A Conversation with Harry Thomas's English Class

Chris Wyrick: Congratulations on the big prize! [the Pulitzer Prize in Poetry for *The Simple Truth* (1994)].

Philip Levine: Well, thank you. Yes. It's been a long time coming. But, you see, patience does pay off. Actually, I think it's better to get it when you're old. Ah, I'm happy to win it.

George Weld: I think now especially a lot of young writers feel a tension between the feeling that they need to be activists in their work for social change and a feeling that, as Auden says, "Poetry makes nothing happen," that poetry is irrelevant or elitist, and I'm wondering whether you feel this tension yourself.

PL: Well, frankly, I think that Auden is wrong. Poetry *does* make things happen. And I think that if a young person is troubled by the idea that he or she is practicing an elitist art, then he or she ought to do something else. I mean, if you have grave doubts about being a poet because you will thereby not achieve your social ambitions, then don't write poetry. Poetry will make it without you. And the question you have to ask yourself is, "Can I make it without poetry?" And if the answer is fuzzy and hazy, do something else. The answer had better be very loud and very clear: "I *can't* make it without poetry." Because there's so much in a life of poetry that can defeat you. And the apparatus for rewarding you is so abysmal, and the rewards themselves, aside from the writing of the poems, so

Held on April 25, 1995, in Harry Thomas's class, English 476, at Davidson College, Davidson, N.C. Published in *Tri-Quarterly* "A Conversation with Harry Thomas's English Class," (winter 1995).

small, that there's no point in doing it unless you're utterly confident that that's your vocation, that's your calling.

When I was your age I had no doubt. I also had social goals, and I was naive enough at eighteen or nineteen to think that poetry or fiction could have a vast social influence because it had a vast influence on the way I felt and thought. It wasn't very long before I realized that if I wasn't being read I wasn't going to influence many people through my writing. I was aware of the fact that while I was reading poets like Eliot, Auden, Spender, Wilfred Owen, Lowell, Stevens, and Hart Crane, my neighbors weren't. They wouldn't have known who the hell I was talking about, so I didn't talk about them. I'd guess much of my family was puzzled. They must have thought, "What is this infatuation and how long will it last?" I was the only member of my family ever to finish college. There's a Yiddish expression that translates, "For this you went to college?" That's exactly what my grandfather said to me when I graduated from college and told him I wanted to be a poet.

Rachel Newcomb: I have another question that's along those same lines. In an interview in 1988 you said that perhaps American poetry had stopped believing in itself, and I was wondering if you felt that contemporary American poetry has become marginal and, if so, how can poetry attract a wider audience?

PL: I don't know why I said that in 1988. I can't recall the occasion. Perhaps I was reading a lot of boring poetry. I talk to a lot of younger poets, and most of them don't seem to feel their generation has found itself as yet. I had a conversation for publication recently with a wonderful younger poet, Kate Daniels—she must be thirty-eight or so—and she felt her generation hadn't yet found what it wanted to do, but she felt that my generation had to assert itself early because we were under the shadows of the giants. If you looked at the magazines in which I first published, you'd see I'm in there with Stevens, Marianne Moore, Williams. I wasn't awed by them. I knew how good they were, I knew they were writing far better than I, but I thought, given enough time, they will vanish from the earth in their bodily incarnations and then maybe my writing will get as good as theirs. Well, the first part did happen, and I'm still waiting for the second.

You asked about the audience for poetry in our country. I think it's the largest it's ever been. I know we're told otherwise. There's this "expert," Joseph Epstein, who published something like "Who Killed Poetry?" Nobody killed poetry. Guys like Epstein like to hearken back to some dreamland America in which people got up in the morning and opened their windows to the birds singing and when they felt their souls elevated they recited American poetry to the waiting world. Bullshit! If you go back to the time when Stevens, Eliot, Williams, were first publishing, exactly the same things were being said in the middlebrow press: "Look at this generation of turkeys. You can't understand a word they write. They're so obscure and so negative. Give us back our uplifting verse!" That was the middlebrow response to one of the great outpourings of poetry in the history of the English language, which took place early in this century. What happened in American poetry was extraordinary: Frost, Stevens, Williams, Pound, Moore, Eliot, all writing at the same time, E. A. Robinson, the whole Imagist thing. And the Epsteins of that hour were griping just as they are now. My guess is that today it still has something to do with class; they can't stand the idea of all these poets coming out of Turkey Tech and Fresno State and Puma J. C. They're from the fancy places that once owned our poetry. We had the same response from the Eastern lords when the Beats hit the press.

I think poetry now is very healthy. You can write about anything. No matter how badly you write you can find somebody who'll publish you. Time will sift the good stuff from the bad. As far as readership goes it's the largest it's ever been.

Patrick Malcor: You said that there is no specific style of poetry right now. Do you think poetry is beyond the point where it can have a movement, a certain mass style, or do you think that it needs that?

PL: There will always be movements. We have one right now that began in California, the Language Poets. Do you know their work? [Blank looks.] You don't, God bless you. Young poets begin movements to have something to belong to, something potentially exciting: "We're going to change American poetry!"

Ever since I began writing I've noticed that certain movements are there mainly to help people without talent write something they can pass off as poetry. If you can't tell a decent story, denounce poems that tell stories. If you can't create characters, denounce poems with people in them. If you can't create images, write boring generalities. If you have no sense of form, imitate the formlessness of the sea. If you have no ear, disparage music. If everything you write is ugly and senseless, remind your readers that the world is ugly and senseless. Bad poets are incredibly resourceful. But those are movements that are easily forgotten. About fifteen years ago we had something called the New Formalism, and it seems to have vanished already. Very curious movement, a sort of nostalgia for the poetry of the 1950s and perhaps for the decade itself, and it occurred at a time when the best formal poets of the 1950s—Wilbur, Merrill, Hecht, Nemerov—were still writing incredibly well. The important movements change the way we see poetry or poetry sees us.

When I was your age a poet friend of mine, Bernie Strempek, and I founded a revolutionary poetry movement. We called it The New Mysticism; that was Bernie's idea. I believe he truly believed in the majesty and burning of the invisible, whereas I was about as mystical as a sofa. Clearly we didn't change anything, not even the way we saw ourselves, but for a few weeks we had great fun talking about how we were going to change the country. Both the Language poets and the New Formalists strike me as less interesting than the New Mystics, though I am hardly objective. They're such conservative movements: neither seems in the least interested in shouldering a social or spiritual or political agenda. Both are academic and largely praised by academic critics and by the poets themselves, but perhaps they will have a healthy impact on our writing. They probably find my work and the contemporary work that resembles it garbage, which is fine. What's important is there is not a single official, accepted style. Today someone entering poetry can take any number of directions and find other poets who will validate his or her work. I hate the notion that any style, mine or anyone else's, is *the* style.

We have had very important, essential movements in this

century. For me the most important one was the Imagist movement, which included such poets as Williams, Pound, Ford Madox Ford, D. H. Lawrence, and profoundly changed both English and American poetry. One in England right after the end of World War II changed the entire focus of their poetry. It was labeled "The Movement" and was something of a repudiation of the high-flown rhetoric of poets like George Barker, Dylan Thomas, and Henry Treece. Suddenly we got these hard-assed poems from poets like Thom Gunn and Philip Larkin. They seemed more interested in what went on in a department store than what went on after you died and went to heaven. They'd write about trying to pick up a girl or spinning out on your motorcycle or finding a pair of pants that made you look sexy. In their poems people sound like people and not holy texts.

And then in the late 1950s we had the Beat and Black Mountain things, all the poets represented in Donald Allen's anthology *The New American Poetry*. If you can still find that book, have a look at it. You'll find it contains some of the best American poets of the second half of the century: Gary Snyder, Creeley, Ginsberg, Robert Duncan, Denise Levertov. All of us who write poetry owe those poets a great debt for ending the absolute domination of the official Eastern establishment; that was a great service.

Todd Cabell: You mention in the first essay in your book, *The Bread of Time,* that anybody can become a poet, that we have democratized poetry, and then you mention creative writing classes in colleges and high schools. I wonder, being a teacher yourself, what exactly do you view as bad in that movement?

PL: Nothing. I think it's a wonderful thing. When I started writing there was not the sense that everybody could become a poet. Chicano poetry did not exist, Asian-American poetry did not exist, such giants as Robert Hayden and Sterling Brown were not represented in the official anthologies. I'm having fun in that essay, and I'm also being serious because I do think there are too many writing programs, and many are staffed by people who can't write themselves. I visit places where poetry writing is taught in graduate programs, and I can't believe the level of writing. Then I see the poetry the teachers write, and I know why. And you visit a class, and everything is praised: the MO seems to be, "Let's pretend all this writing is poetry." Once you create a program you require students, so you let everyone in, and you keep them in by making them happy. I also visit writing programs in which real standards are operating, the students have talent and are reading and working like mad; the teachers are dedicated, demanding, fair, and they are gifted and productive poets themselves. There are two things you must have for a valuable writing program: first and most important, the right students. Then the teachers. You could have mediocre teachers if you had great students because the students will teach each other and inspire each other. The problem is great students rarely gravitate to mediocre teachers.

Chris Wyrick: I'd like to ask a question about your method of writing. In *What Work Is,* in the poem "Scouting," you say, "I'm scouting, getting the feel of the land," and in the poem "What Work Is," "Forget you. This is about waiting, shifting from one foot to another." And I want to ask you if you could tell us more about this process of scouting that you engage in your poems.

PL: That's a difficult and interesting question. How do you research a poem, which is what scouting is? Or at least that's one of the things I'm scouting for in the poem, the poem itself. You know you're constantly obliged when you apply for grants or things like grants to describe the specific steps you're going to take to write the book you're asking for financial support to write, and of course you rarely know exactly what you'll have to do. I'd call it a kind of scouting. It's a circling and circling, quite literally—a cityscape, a landscape, a subject, an emotional obsession. I'll give you an example. I have this fascination with Spanish anarchism, so back in the 1970s I went to one of the great collections of anarchist literature, the International Institute for Social Study in Amsterdam. The records of the CNT and the FAI—the National Workers Confederation and the Iberian Anarchist Federation—were stored there. Most of the stuff is in Spanish, and at the time my Spanish was good enough to read it. The people who worked in the library there were very helpful and generous; they brought me whatever I wanted to see, old newspapers, posters, memoirs, manifestoes, anything I asked for, and I sat there for hours, day after day, reading. The poetry I finally got had nothing to do with Spanish anarchism, though I have written many poems out of that obsession; this "scouting" produced poems that had to do with being in a library. They had to do with the quality of light, the sadness that invades a library late in the afternoon when you've been there all day from 9:00 in the morning until 5:30 and suddenly you realize the light has changed and the day is ending. In Amsterdam the weather can change very suddenly, and I would glance out the window and dark clouds were blowing in from the North Sea, and the day was totally different from the one I left when I entered the library. My heart was always yearning to go out in the streets and to be in Amsterdam; it's such a beautiful and lively city. I learned a hell of a lot about Spanish anarchism, and I wrote about my hours in the library, the people I met there, the yearning for the city, the shocking realization of how quickly time was passing and the light going.

And "Scouting," the poem itself, is about my days in North Carolina, your dear state, where I lived the summer of 1954 in a mountain town called Boone. I thought I'd made a drastic step that might mean I would never become the amazing poet I had seemed destined to become. I had just gotten married. I had fallen in love with a woman who had a young child, and so we married. I thought, "Look what a foolish thing love has driven me to do. I must now be a responsible human being. I'm only twenty-six years old and I've thrown my young life away." You know, men at twenty-six are total idiots. I would go for long walks most days. I didn't have to work, my new wife was working and supporting all of us. I was supposed to be writing poems, but my mother-in-law had come for the wedding, and no one can write with his mother-in-law in the house, even, as in my case, if she's a lovely woman. So I went on these long walks and began to discover the landscape of those mountains and the people. I'd knock on the doors of these little cabins and say, "Could I have a drink of water?" And besides the water, which I always got, I'd get different responses. "Where you from, son?" "What are you doing here?" They'd hear my accent and know I was not local, these gracious country people sharing their water with me, their time; we'd have wonderful conversations. It was a kind of scouting. As I got further and further into it I realized I was carrying out research, I was researching myself as well as these people and their place. My mother-in-law left, so in the mornings I'd work for hours on poetry; I found Saintsbury's *History of English Prosody* in the local library, never had been read, pages uncut, and I poured over that. I'd been trying to write poetry for ten years, and I still didn't know how to do it and knew I didn't know. But I was getting clues, and I was also learning how to research poems: you keep your eyes open, your ears open, all your senses open. The world responds to you, and you respond to the world. It goes on that way, it never ends.

I've been very lucky. I've never had one of those terrible droughts. Three or four months is the longest I've ever gone without writing poetry or something I could regard as poetry. I've come to think part of the process, an essential part, is waiting, being patient, and avoiding what one might call busy-work. There's the temptation to construct what you secretly know is second-rate and keep working at it because it beats not working at anything. I think you're better off not writing at all than just soothing yourself with busywork. I'm not talking about beginning writers; they have no idea where anything will go and should plow ahead with whatever comes to them. By the time you've been at it fifteen years you know when you're just imitating yourself.

"Scouting" is also about that dreadful moment here in North Carolina when I said to myself, "Philip, you have o'erstepped your usual timidity and entered upon marriage." You know I was just like any other jerk my age. No one had told me how to become a poet, and I'd figured out that if you didn't have money there were two ways to live: you can have a family or you can write poetry, but you ain't going to do both. How the hell are you going to take care of kids, help dress and feed them, get them off to school, and then write a poem? What kind of nonsense is that? I figured I should have someone coming into my study with toast and tea, I should have silence interrupted at intervals for wonderful meals. Wasn't that how Rilke lived? How many nights do you think he sat up with a sick kid? You know at one point or another in your life you have to wake up and become a person. The irony of all this is I was incredibly lucky. I was marrying a woman who had a profound regard for poetry, and this kid I adopted turned out to be one of my best friends. It was probably one of the three or four intelligent decisions I've made in my whole life. Another was buying the house I work in in Fresno. Another was not going to the Korean War. I can't think of another one, but there must be a fourth.

Mary Stephens: I'm interested in how memory works in the writing process because so many of your poems are retrospective. How does this process differ from poems that are observed at the moment of conception? And how important is looking back, not only on your own experiences but on your earlier writing?

PL: I don't know if I can answer the second part. It seems to me that you made a distinction between writing a poem that would come out of memory and one that would come out of an experience that was before you. But you'll notice that in my poems it almost doesn't seem to matter what's before me: I go back into memory and try often to twine what I remember with what I'm observing. And I'm not sure why I do this, although it's obviously something that I do. I think that a lot of it has to do with the fact that I feel an urgency to record things because they seem so transitory. And I am now a kind of archive of people, places, and things that no longer exist. I carry them around with me, and if I get them on paper I give them at least some existence. And that seems like a legitimate thing to be doing with poetry. To be granting some form of permanence—I mean, however permanent the poems are— to the things, to a way of life and the people who made up that way of life.

As far as looking back at my own writing, I try not to. I purposely don't memorize my poems. When I'm on the brink of memorizing a poem I stop using it at readings. I wait for time to erase it because I don't want to memorize it.

Geordie Schimmel: What if not poetry? If not the dialogue with stars and trees at thirteen, what would you have chosen?

PL: It would have been the dialogue at fourteen. That's what I was going to do. I don't have the least doubt about it. Before I was ten I was utterly fascinated with language, with the shape and flavor of words. And I got so much pleasure out of using language, and I used it with snap. Besides, there weren't that many other options. I couldn't have been a dancer, I'm too awkward. I can't draw so I couldn't have been a painter. Maybe an Abstract Expressionist, except my sense of color stinks. I can't carry a tune worth a damn, so although I love music it wasn't for me. I might have become a critic. No, never a *cricket,* as Mark Twain calls them. Better to be an honest huckster and sell Buicks. I might have become a novelist. When I was in college I worked as hard at fiction as I did at poetry, but back then my temperament wasn't suited for it; I hadn't yet developed the incredible patience a novelist requires.

William Robert: I'd like to return to your works for a minute and ask you a question about them. Pretty consistently, from the earliest ones to the ones that just came out in *The Simple Truth,* you develop many philosophical threads. And one of the most fundamental seems to me to be the lack of, the impotency of, even the impossibility of, true communication between individuals. Do you see this as an ironic stance for a poet, namely one who depends on communication, to take?

PL: No. No, I don't. Failing to communicate is part of what we live with, part of our condition. Poetry is about as good as we can get at communicating without the aid of gestures, without the aid of our bodies. Rilke wrote somewhere that without our bodies we cannot love. Also with our bodies, with our gestures, with our facial expressions, we can communicate far more fully than with merely words on the telephone or words in a letter. Poetry is as close as we can get to complete communication with words alone. And I think it's good enough. The miracle of poetry is that it can cross so many barriers. Approximate communication seems so amazing itself when you consider how separate we are or how separate we have conceived of ourselves. I believe that we aren't nearly as separate as we think we are. If, for example, someone in this room were running a fever we would all heat up a bit, we'd feel it even though we might not know we felt it. Our eyes tell us we're more separate than we actually are, and our conscious experience tells us, and we've conditioned ourselves to believe we're more separate. But to get back to poetry, given who we've created out of ourselves, poetry is miraculous.

But you're right: there is an obsession in much of my work with the failures of people to communicate, but those failures are usually very specific. I'm usually concerned with a few people, perhaps only two, and how they fail to communicate. A book that moved me enormously when I was young, maybe eighteen, was *Winesburg, Ohio*. I remember a story about two very lonely people, a man and a woman, who have no one to communicate with and whose experience of love is very limited. As I recall—I haven't read the story in ages—they get together and they discover they have these mutual needs and they could be dear friends. The man oversteps the bounds of this budding friendship; while the woman is trying to speak out of her joy that she has a listener he shuts her up by kissing her. There's this awful and wonderful irony that he has chosen to communicate his love or joy in the occasion this way, and she wants to communicate it another way, and you can't do both at the same time.

Kristina Nevius: Through this interview you've mentioned languages. What effect have foreign languages and cultures had on your poetry?

PL: When I go to a foreign country where I don't speak the language I usually make no effort to learn it. I'm just "The Ugly American," as Eugene Burdick called us in his novel years ago. I enjoy the ignorance, I use it. Say I go into the Campo Fiori, the great open market in Rome. I stop and listen to two people standing in line to buy eggs. The man says to the woman, "Was there ever a more perfect shape than an egg? And the luminosity! The amazing delicacy of the color, the way it takes the hues of the air. Not only does the egg contain sustenance for us, for our bodies which feed our souls, but within each egg is the potential of a creature that can fly." Amazing, they say such rare things in such common places in Rome; Italians are angels. Of course that's not what they're saying at all. The guy has turned to his cousin Elfonzina and said, "Holy shit, the bastard raised the price again!" Because I don't speak Italian I've endowed him with poetry, and I say to myself, "How fortunate you are, Philip, to be living among such profound people when in fact they're saying the same trivial things they'd be saying in Fresno or Detroit."

One invaluable thing I learned from studying Spanish was how great our own poetry is, how many things it can do that Spanish poetry hasn't yet done. We appear in American poetry and we speak in our daily voices. It gave me a new regard for American poetry. Discovering the great poetry written in Spanish in this century was intoxicating. There's also much more awful poetry written in Spain than in the U.S. because anyone who goes to the university in Spain publishes a book of poetry. The dentist will hand you a beautifully printed book of poems—each dentist has one—all about the perfume of flowers, the brightness of the moon, the tenderness of kisses, the sweetness of the night air of Andalusia, the kindness of wild herbs. The poetry of love, dreams, moonlight, fantasy.

I think, too, it's very good to read poetry in another language to discover the immense possibilities we're not taking advantage of in our poetry. I know you can discover much of that reading translations, say of Zbigniew Herbert or Tömas Tranströmer, but I think you get an even keener sense when you read someone like García Lorca or César Vallejo in the original. And you're inspired in the same way you're inspired when you read Whitman or Dickinson or Williams. I can still recall struggling with the poems of Miguel Hernández in the original and those sudden glimpses of how astonishing the poetry was, how brutal and lyrical at exactly the same moment. I'd never read anything like it; it reconfirmed my belief in the power and beauty of poetry in the face of the worst life can dish out. These are poems that grew out of the most tragic circumstances. They are full of indescribable pain, which he foresees. They are very great and very difficult poems; I had to work hours, and then I would get this glimpse of their majesty.

Alex Crumbley: Did it take you long to become comfortable writing persona poems? And when you do, do you have trouble with people assuming you're the narrator when you're not?

PL: First thing, it didn't take long at all. Once I decided I wanted to do it, I just did it. I had written a lot of fiction, at least a dozen stories and large chunks of two novels, so I was used to the problem of getting into the heads of other characters and getting them to speak in my writing.

As far as people misreading, I don't much care. I remember a review I got, I think it was in the *Village Voice,* in which a woman wrote that one of my poems from *7 Years from Somewhere* was very curious. The poem, "I Could Believe," is in the voice of a guy who has come back from the Spanish Civil War. This woman wrote something like, "Levine is an autobiographical poet, so it's amazing to discover that he fought in the Spanish Civil War, which ended when he was eleven." She mused over this, and then wrote, "Perhaps he's trying something different."

Even our fellow poets and friends read our poetry differently. I remember going to a class at the University of Minnesota and having a conversation with the students; it was much like today. At the end someone asked if I would read one poem. I said, "Sure, let me read something I'm working on and we'll see what you think of it." I read "Listen Carefully" in an early draft. After I was done a young woman asked me if I would publish the poem. I said, "Yeah, if I ever get it right." "But if your sister read it, how would she feel?" I said, "I don't have a sister." She was shocked. My host, Michael Dennis Browne, an English poet who has become a fine American poet, then told an interesting story.

He said, "You know, Sharon Olds was sitting in that same chair last year, and for some reason she got on the subject of Phil's poetry. She told us how she had asked Phil where she might get 'chocolate cookies in the shape of Michigan,' cookies Phil refers to in one of his poems. To Sharon's surprise Phil said he just made it up." Michael quoted her in a surprised voice, "He made it up!" as though that were unheard of. Sharon is a dear friend of mine, and my guess is she was having fun. It's very possible it's not something she would do in her own poems, but I'm sure she knows it's something I do all the time. To me it's always open house; if you want it and it doesn't exist, just make it up. This poem with the cookies in it is about an amazing kid, a kid so amazing he's not human and yet he is. He's what human beings would be if human beings were totally themselves.

That's what poets live for, those days when we are totally ourselves. I know when I'm there. I awaken in the morning, and I know I'm there, that today it's going to happen. I've been working toward that day for ages, and when it comes I'm in no hurry. Take your time, move around, absorb all you can, reach out as far as possible. You're not going to lose it. It's there. It's you.

A Conversation with Kate Daniels
and Craig Watson

Philip Levine: I wonder if you get a sense of strength from the fact that you're writing at a time when people your age are defining a generation's poetry and are doing it well. Do you feel you belong to something that's significant?

Kate Daniels: God, what if I say no? Isn't that awful?

PL: It'll be the truth.

KD: The answer is no. (*Laughs.*) I don't know if I want it to be in print. I don't live my life with a consciousness of being part of a generation.

PL: How old are you now?

KD: Forty-one.

PL: I don't think I got the sense I belonged to a generation until I was older than you.

KD: You belonged to a very different generation. Yours overthrew something and had to go through great struggles to do it. I'm not part of anything like that. The biggest thing poets of my generation grapple with is how to line themselves up with neoformalism or something like that. It's not the same as dealing with the New Criticism or T. S. Eliot, Pound, Williams and all those people still alive when you were a younger poet starting out.

PL: When I first started publishing I was in the same magazines as Pound, Williams, Stevens. Later the Vietnam War tended to bring us together as a generation.

KD: The writing community today is so un-homogeneous.

Held at Vanderbilt University (spring 1995). Published in the *Vanderbilt Review,* "Conversation with Kate Daniels," 1995.

So many different kinds of poets have access to publication. I don't think that was as true when you were a young poet.

PL: It wasn't true at all.

KD: Yeah, I know. I was just being polite. There's less a sense now that there are literary gods who must be worshiped or equaled or genuflected in front of; all the gods are different for each literary community.

PL: People ask if that's a good thing or a bad thing. I don't know. I found that what I grew up with wasn't that comfortable. There were so few poets around, but on the other hand if you published a book you didn't tend to get lost. It meant more than it does now.

KD: My own feeling is that today it's probably better than it was in your time. Nothing can enrage me more than to read some elitist who's decided who should be able to write and what that person should be able to say. It's un-American to me.

PL: It's indecent. It's what we . . .

KD: It's indecent. You're right.

PL: It's what we do for ourselves. Each of us does it separately. We know when we start we have a right to write, and then we try to do it as best we can. You got a question?

Craig Watson: Related to what you just said, I was thinking about the audience. I saw Rita Dove on a cable channel giving a lecture, and she suggested having poetry videos instead of MTV to broaden the audience of poetry. I was wondering if that should be a concern. There's been all this talk about specialization of poetry and that only poets read poetry. How do you accomplish that broadening of the audience?

PL: I wouldn't wish it on any poet. It's so hard to get something down on a page that satisfies you, something intelligent and original and perhaps even beautiful, that if you're also going to concern yourself with making it available to everybody on MTV, forget it. I'd be crushed before I started. We've already got MTV, and I don't see the point of going into competition with it. Or even trying to get on it. We practice another art, an art that has never been as popular as what's on MTV. I fell in love with poetry, not MTV.

KD: These calls to make poetry more available seem to me to have something to do with what I was saying before about the fact there are all these different sorts of people writing poetry now. There is an enormous amount of poetry activity, and there has been since the 1960s. It's very different from what Phil was talking about earlier when you published your first book, in the 1940s or 1950s, and you got reviewed in the *Times* and the *Herald Tribune* and *Time* plus all the literary journals. All this other stuff was not going on. Even here in Nashville they have these poetry jams, open mike readings, encounters between musicians and poets. Where do they want poetry to go? Brodsky wants it to be on the supermarket stands next to the *National Enquirer* and in hotel rooms. Who do they think is going to read it, or are they really bemoaning the fact that not as many people as they'd like are reading a certain kind of poetry?

PL: I remember going to MIT to hear Theodore Roethke read—maybe it was 1952—and twelve people showed. Today a poet with that reputation would draw five hundred.

KD: I have a question. Your poetry was some of the first contemporary poetry I read and loved, and when I began reading it and was much younger I suppose I loved it for its subject matter. It was something I could relate to, having grown up in the working class. I suppose I loved it also for its narrative style, but as I've gotten older and you've gotten older, I now feel that the thing I really love is the way your poems can be so narrative and then with very little preparation or warning evolve into something that is nonnarrative— that is so lyrical. It's not something I see in the poetry of other people. There's a way in which other people who write a kind of narrative verse will all of a sudden pull the rabbit out of the hat and there will be some, you know, lyric shindig at the end to try to get out of the poem. But you don't do that. You move back and forth, and it's all sort of one. It's amazing how you do it because I have an imagination that is so relentlessly narrative and linear. I wonder how that works in your poems. I wonder what it's like to see through your eyes. For example, when I look at a painting, my eyes feel like they're going to blow up and fall out, trying to make visual sense of the piece. The stories are springing up in my head. I cannot ever get away from being narrative. Metaphors have to hit me over the head for them to get into my poetry. What's it like for you? How do you see? How do you see the settings in your poems? Does this make sense?

PL: To tell you the truth, I don't know how I do it. I know it's a very common thing for me to have two movies going on in my head at the same time. And they keep twining around each other.

KD: They're the same poem, the same movie, but they're different versions?

PL: No, they're different movies. I'll associate one with the other, and then I'll cross them.

KD: While you're writing?

PL: While I'm just thinking or walking along or anything. While I'm dreaming. My dreams seem intertwined with different narrative elements. I remember having a conversation with Charles Wright, who says he can't write narrative at all. He asked me what my dreams were like, and when I said they were separate stories, he said, "They're stories, but they're stories!" I said, "Yeah, events that happen sequentially." That didn't happen to him. I'm sure it happens to you.

KD: What's it like when you go to a museum and look at a painting you've never seen before? Let's say it's a fairly abstract work, what's it like?

PL: I'm not nuts about abstract work, but let's say I saw a Hopper I never saw before. I'd probably make a narrative around it.

KD: What would you do with it?

PL: First I'd regard it formally. I'd study the light, I'd try to get the quality of the motion. For example, if a dog was coming in from one side of the painting, I'd wonder whose dog it was. Does it mean someone not in the painting is coming in and the dog is coming in ahead of that person? If a man and woman were in the painting I'd wonder why one was closer to me than the other, why one has turned a shoulder toward the other. I'd try to define the relationships. I'd be concerned about class. I'd study their dress, how much skin was showing, did Hopper lust after the women, did he envy the men. I'd make a movie out of it.

KD: What about photography. In your poems sometimes

there's a photographic clarity, and then it's just gone, and a moment later it's back.

PL: I'm fascinated by photography. As a teenager I had a camera. My brother and I built a darkroom and developed and printed our own work. You could buy a decent German camera for fifteen bucks; you could buy 35-mm film in bulk and cut it up. It was very inexpensive. We'd go out into the city and take all these pictures and then wonder, What have I got in this camera? I'd go home and put it through the developer and look at the little negatives, make contact prints, and there was nothing there. We'd enlarge the negatives, frame them, and the stuff was still no good. I think we both had very corny taste. I'm still mad for photography, and for that reason I've put a lot of photographs on the covers of my books. Sheeler's on *Tom Jefferson,* Louis Hine on *What Work Is,* and the famous one on *Sweet Will,* the one who did the book with Agee.

KD: Walker Evans.

PL: Yeah. "Joe's Auto Graveyard" is his. I grew up with photographs like that, and that was photography to me. Those photographs of people or dramatic rural or urban landscapes excited the hell out of me, and when I was young I thought, I'd love to get those people and those landscapes into my poems. Maybe I did.

KD: You did. What do you think of the photographs of Sally Mann?

PL: Don't know her work.

KD: There's been a big brouhaha about her work. She takes photographs of her children that are highly sexualized, very suggestive, some people think pornographic. Others find her work brilliant. I find it disturbing.

PL: I hate much of the work of Diane Arbus. It's more than just condescending; it's savage.

CW: I was thinking about Adrienne Rich and her struggle with the question of how to use people close to you in your poems, her anger at Robert Lowell for the way he used his wife and the divorce. Where do you draw the line in using people you know in your poetry?

PL: If I left my wife I sure as hell wouldn't write about it and publish the stuff. Actually I might write about it, but I'd never publish it. I even disguise the people in my family. Of course your relatives are likely to enter your poems, but they don't have to do it in their own names and in their own costumes. I'm for protecting the guilty. I don't think what Lowell did was daring. It says, This is real, you must have an emotional response to it. How do you feel?

KD: It's an interesting and complicated question. I think poets of my generation do it a lot without even being conscious of it. Not exactly what Lowell did, but many contemporary poets use autobiographical material in ways that are barely changed. I realize you're not just talking about using autobiographical material.

PL: Selecting the prurient elements.

KD: When I was moved to write about some very autobiographical, very personal material in my life, the death of a child in my family, it never occurred to me beforehand that I would write about it. I began to write about the myth of Niobe, and then I realized I was writing about the other thing—my personal story. That didn't feel invasive to me, it didn't feel violating. It's not clear to me what other people think. Maybe it was indecent and unfeeling of me to write about a tragedy that affected me but also affected other people as well. Right now I'm about to finish this book that has Simone Weil as the main character, and so I think about this. Can I do that, can I use this character?

PL: Of course you can.

KD: Of course I can. (*Laughs.*) You're not talking about who *you* can have in your poems, but how will you treat them when they enter or how will you treat their story.

PL: Yeah, but she belongs to history. You can't hurt Simone Weil. I might write a different poem about Simone Weil and take her to task for her self-righteousness. And you might make a hero out of her. She's part of our culture, part of our history. I read your Niobe book, and I was very moved. You were taking specifics and getting at universal suffering; I thought it was a powerful book. When you told me you were writing it I thought, Oh, God, don't write that.

KD: I told you I was going to write it?

PL: You wrote and said you wanted to send it to me, and I thought, Oh, no! I thought it would be a disaster.

KD: Oh ye of little faith!

PL: Yes, well it's not something I could have done. That's really what I was telling myself. When I got it I was truly moved by the book; you'd merged the specific with the mythic.

KD: I couldn't have done it by writing about it directly. I had to have some device to distance myself from the material. The material was too hard, too painful for me.

CW: (*to Levine*) You must think about the self on these terms too; you've got many poems in which you create a new self—this is the theme of *One for the Rose,* especially in a poem like "I Was Born in Lucerne."

PL: I announce in that poem what I'm doing in the book. I'm making up new lives for myself. My own seems ordinary, boring, so why not take some others? I've always felt that way. Why restrict myself to what happened to me? I'm liable to invent anything, so why not do that in my poetry?

KD: Let me ask you a hard question. How old are you now?

PL: Sixty-seven.

KD: What's it like to write poems now?

PL: A little harder than it was at fifty. I think I wrote best from about age forty-seven or eight to fifty-four or five. I started losing creative energy somewhere in my mid-fifties; I think from my late forties until then I still had as much creative energy as I'd ever had and at the same time I seemed more competent. Now I'm surprised when I go off on a new thing, and the whole thing is not as worrisome; my guess is that if what I've written so far doesn't amount to anything then what I write from now on won't make any difference.

KD: When you were younger did you write with a plan? I'm forty-one, and I've been seriously writing for twenty years. If somebody asked what my plan is I couldn't say, but I have some intuitive sense of how what I write is developing and where I want to go, which means I must have some goal for it somewhere. Did you have that, and if you did do you still—you never did? You just kind of make it up every day as you go?

PL: Yeah, I actually believe in that. I believe a plan is a mistake, for me. At first I suffered because I couldn't find a plan, and—

KD: That's a great line. "At first I suffered because I couldn't find a plan . . ."

PL: And I was scorned because I couldn't. I was in college with people who were going to be linguists or scientists or philosophers, and they all had a vision of the world. They would berate me because I was confused about everything. It was only later that I realized that the confusion was a source of poetry and that not having a plan opened me up to all sorts of possibilities that would otherwise have been closed. They'd decided what meant what whereas I had to keep searching, which kept taking me to material I could use for poetry. In my thirties I realized I hadn't been at a disadvantage. In fact it may have been what I was meant to be, a poet without a plan.

KD: But at some point, you must concede, you had a project, whether you were undertaking it consciously or not—

PL: I could see the past was leading me to something.

KD: That's what I'm talking about. Do you see that now.

PL: Oh, sure.

KD: Now you do? Okay.

PL: I remember how, when people started to define me I protested against it. Maybe fifteen years ago I wrote a poem in which I prayed to die in Barcelona. I'd gone back to the city I'd loved even under Franco. He was gone, but the place was still a circus of misery: the unemployed everywhere, junkies, alcoholics, the homeless. It was as though now that they didn't have a fascist state to crush them they decided to crush themselves. There was nothing I could offer these people, and so back in Fresno I wrote this miserable poem and showed it to my wife and my best friend, Peter Everwine, a wonderful poet. They both said to me, "That's not you. You don't pray to die. You're a real survivor." I said, "Fuck you, I wrote the poem, who are you to tell me who I am?" For fifteen minutes I was pissed off. I remember when my book *1933* came out and got bad reviews Jane Cooper said to me, "Don't pay any attention to those reviews. They're bad because you're doing something you're not supposed to do. You're supposed to be angry, fire-eating, and now you're unashamedly crying over the suffering of your family. Other poets cry over their families, but you don't, so get back to your own territory, to your working-class revolutions."

KD: That's very astute.

CW: I have another question about your other work, which is teaching. I was wondering if you would comment on the strange relationship between creative writing programs and the rest of the English Department with the rise of theory.

KD: It's stranger in some places than in others. I'm not a writer who's opposed to those theoretical ways of thinking. One thing it does is push writers, who are generally liberal and open-minded, into affiliation with academic colleagues who are politically very conservative. I saw that happen at a school I was teaching at not long ago. I was the creative writing representative on a committee to revise the undergraduate curriculum. There was a portion of the mission statement that said, basically, we agree we teach books or texts, and we agree that texts have authors. I missed a meeting, and when I came back it had changed into we agree texts are authored by persons, processes, or cultures, and I went completely crazy. I said, "If this stands we'll have to get T-shirts for all the creative writers that say, 'I have authored my own text and I am a person, not a process or a culture.'"

PL: What surprises me often is that when I meet these people and talk to them about baseball or the baseball strike or the O.J. trial or the best wine store, they seem friendly, human, they drink, they eat, they advise me on wine, but when we draw closer to the arena of the text they become rabid. I wonder where is that person I was just talking to. When I was a student this happened in philosophy. I was studying Plato, Kant, Hegel, Aristotle, and these Logical Positivists came along, and they wanted to burn the old books. And I was into aesthetics, which they didn't even think existed. These may be the same people with face-lifts and better tailors.

KD: Another anecdote from another school I taught at. I remember the *New York Times* ran an article in which Jay McInerny recounted an event from a Raymond Carver class. There was one Ph.D. student in with the creative writers; the class was called Form and Theory of the Short Story. This Ph.D. student had been showing increasing signs of anxiety and irritation at the way the class just read stories and talked about them the way writers do. Finally he raised his hand and said, "Professor Carver, I don't understand what's going on in this class. It's called Form and Theory of the Short Story." Professor Carver just sat back for a minute and said, "Well, the way I look at it is this way. We read the story and then you form your own theory." At the time I was teaching in this new MFA program, and the creative writing students were having a difficult time with the whole critical theory component of the department. I used to post things on my door all the time, and I posted this article. Well, a young colleague who was a critical theorist showed up at my door and wanted to challenge me to a duel. He inquired if I was aware that I had insulted every single junior faculty member. My response was, "Are you seeking to censor my free expression? It's for my students, it's a funny anecdote, and it relates to their experiences." A sense of humor is sorely lacking.

CW: I have one more about political poetry. You wrote about this in an essay called "Part of the Problem," where you defended Adrienne Rich from Helen Vendler and Marjorie Perloff. A number of critics and poets look at the Vietnam War years and see all the bad poems that were written and complain about the period. I was wondering if either of you could speak about the distinctions between good and bad political poetry, if there are certain different choices you make as you write a political poem that you keep in mind.

PL: I doubt it. They had a right to complain about the bad war poetry. I refused to let some of my own stuff be anthologized. I read it years later and thought it was junk. We had the best motives: Let's stop burning Asians, let's stop burning people of color in our own country. The best motives aren't enough. Duncan has a long antiwar poem that really works. It's quite amazing; his artistry was not lacking. Most of us had the best will in the world, we had a charge of emotion, and we had the imagery off the TV screen.

KD: I love what I think we all mean when we say political poetry, some of the poetry that has been most important to me is by people like Nazim Hikmet and Miklos Radnoti. I tend to think that most poems written at any given time are mediocre, so it doesn't surprise me that a lot of the Sixties poetry wasn't very good. I was a kid then, but it seems to me that it was a very wild, changing, opening time and that everything was up for grabs, including how you write a poem and what makes poetry. We are so American, we will invent a new kind of potato chip or a new kind of poetry. Maybe that's part of it. I'm never hard on anyone who wants to write political poetry. Some of my favorite poets are the contemporary Swedish poets, who are profoundly, irrevocably, relentlessly political. I love their work.

PL: Take the poetry of the Spanish Civil War. You look at the work of John Cornford and the other young English poet who went there and died, Julian Bell, and Spender and Auden, and you compare their work to what Vallejo wrote; they're worlds apart. The poems of Miguel Hernández and Vallejo are just unbelievably great, and the other poems are interesting. There's a way in which it's an exotic world to the Englishmen. To the Peruvian and the Spaniard it's just the world and they're at home in it and they know all about that kind of rage and that kind of exploitation and the endless suffering of those without. That's what they write out of. These upper-middle-class people coming from Oxford and Cambridge, they were wonderful people with the best intentions in the world . . .

KD: So where does that leave Americans? It's like we've got a literary establishment that doesn't want to give much credence to expression from our own battlefronts. You know what I mean?

PL: Yeah.

KD: It's just batted down time and again. This isn't poetry. Who killed poetry? Where does that leave us?

PL: There is an academic, elitist, conservative conspiracy to deny the validity of this poetry. We've had it for ages. Look at what's happened to McGrath's "Letter to an Imaginary Friend." It's extraordinary, our "Canto General," and nobody pays any attention to it. I recently discovered the University of Illinois is embarking on a whole series of books of

American political poetry. The first book is by Edwin Rolfe, a guy who went to Spain with the Lincoln Brigade. They're starting with him, and I guess they're going to come forward toward the present, maybe toward the future. I have the feeling the poetry exists, that it's always being written. It's just being denied.

An Interview with Kate Bolick

Philip Levine's first poems emerged, unwritten, the year he turned thirteen and started talking to the moon. After the dinner dishes were washed and dried, he would roam the deserted streets of Detroit and pour forth his rambling utterances, making and remaking what he hoped were poems. "Once the dark took over, nothing was impossible," he wrote in his 1994 autobiography, *The Bread of Time.* "Each night that I labored joyously at my new craft and art, I sang out to the city and the larger world beyond the city, and no one was the wiser."

That same year, Levine got his first job—as a jewelry store gofer—and spent the rest of his summers, until he finished high school, working in factories and on construction crews. As a student at Detroit's Wayne University, he worked part-time year round, reading textbooks during his lunch breaks and continuing to craft poems. A few years after graduating from college, however, he made an essential discovery. In order to write poems that would "outlast [his] own body," as he recounts in his autobiography, he needed to devote himself to poetry with "unequaled ferocity." And so, at age twenty-six, he punched his last time card, packed up his suitcase, and headed off to the Iowa Writer's Workshop.

It's been forty-six years since Levine quit industrial work, but the people and places of his midcentury Detroit continue to shape his sensibility. Memories of shops and factories like Feinberg and Breslin's First-Rate Plumbing and Plating, Chevrolet Gear and Axle, and Detroit Transmission crackle through his conversations and emerge in his poems bristling with details—the stubborn grease, the salted onions for dinner, the

From *DoubleTake* (winter 2001).

bitter fumes of a pickling tank. "Everything," he writes in the poem "Magpiety," "is speaking or singing / We're still here." Indeed, Levine may have been hampered by a sore throat when we met last summer in his home in Brooklyn, but his memories and animated stories were irrepressible; by the time the afternoon was spent—taking with it a pocketful of lozenges—the room was fairly crowded with conjured presences.

What kind of jobs did you have when you were young? What was your attitude toward them?

The first job I ever got was in 1941, when I was thirteen. I worked in a vast jewelry store in downtown Detroit where they sold all kinds of fancy baubles. I was a gofer. A woman would come in with a brooch and ask how much it would cost to have it fixed, and I'd race up to the attic and present the problem to the jewelers, get the answer, and race down. Someone would come in to buy something pricey and present a check, and I'd be assigned to race to his bank to find out if he was good for it. Mainly I just ran. I felt like what I was, a nonentity. I learned a couple things: no one trusts anyone's word, and in order to keep a job, even a lousy one, you have to do what you're told and pretend you like it. And you have to keep your mouth shut.

When I was fourteen, I got a better-paying job, in a factory that made soap chips. It was a disgusting place. Every Monday morning, these huge black barrels would be delivered—the sort in which you would expect to find used motor oil—filled with animal fat from cheap restaurants. By some process I never understood, the fat was transformed into blocks of soap, and then the blocks were shaved into these charming curlicues, and my task was to wheel these racks of curlicues into a drying room, where they were transformed into soap chips that were boxed and sold to laundries. The drying room was a scary place, windowless, the color of dirty aluminum, airless, and incredibly hot. If you were in there more than fifteen seconds the sweat would burst out all over you, either from the heat or pure fear. I timed the drying and then wheeled the racks out. Sometimes the racks would break, and I'd have the job of making new ones. To do this, I got to work outside, which was wonderful, especially if the weather was good. I'd hammer the wooden frames together and feel like I was making something, like I was a working man, a person.

A year later, I worked for my grandfather in his "grease shop," which is what they called such places in Detroit. It was a small place, maybe employed a dozen people, half of them women, reconditioning used auto parts. My grandfather didn't treat me any differently from anyone else that worked for him, which was badly. I liked him anyway. He was a real lesson on how to survive in America.

What was your grandfather's story? What did he teach you?

He'd come to America from Russia around 1905 with a younger brother. They were in their twenties and on the run from the Russo-Japanese War. Some people from his village had settled in Detroit, so that's where they came. The two got jobs on the night shift at a stove factory near the Detroit River. They were small men, and the work was very difficult. The brother so hated it he decided to go back to Russia and face the music. My grandfather was stubborn and very willful, and he hung on. He was a real study in perseverance, in overcoming terrible odds. He never learned to read or write English. He told me later that when he came to the States he knew two languages, Yiddish and Russian, but by the time he was sixty he could barely read either. As the grandfather of a growing kid, he was a dream. He loved women, good food, booze. He'd gamble everything on a brainstorm, and sometimes he lost everything. He'd just start over. He wanted to live large, and he did. He was a lesson: you only get one life, so use it. If other people didn't like it, tough.

How did your attitude toward work change as you got older?

As a kid, I was very small and skinny. I found it much harder to do some of the work than the bigger guys did. As I got older, I felt I needed more money—the whole thing of taking out girls entered my life—and so I took factory jobs, and often the work was physically overwhelming. Back then, nothing was automated: if you loaded a truck or a railroad car, you did it by hand. At about the age of seventeen, I began to grow to my present, magnificent height of five foot ten, and my weight began to crawl up from 135 toward 160, and I started to gain real strength from these jobs. At age twenty-two, I was 185—the heaviest and strongest I've ever been. I was working on road construction, US 24, swinging a sledge-hammer and breaking up concrete with a jackhammer. My body had adapted to the work that I once found so punishing, and now the work almost became pleasurable, the way difficult exercise can be. Perhaps because this strength was so long in coming, I took great joy from it. But there was no mental growth in that sort of brute labor, and in that way it was killing. As I look back on it, I can almost see that aspect as a plus: because my mind wasn't involved, it was free to roam where it wanted. I had to be attentive to a degree so as not to mangle a hand, but mainly I let my mind wander into poetry and music. In the factories, I could recite poems to my heart's content and no one would hear me, and almost all of us sang in our lousy voices. I invented my own terrible poems and declaimed them, and I butchered the songs I loved.

During the winter of 1953, you were twenty-five and working at Chevrolet Gear and Axle. You were also writing poetry. "I believed even then that if I could transform my experience into poetry," you wrote in The Bread of Time, *"I would give it the value and dignity it did not begin to possess on its own." What do you remember about this?*

When I first got a job in an auto factory, I must have been eighteen or so—it was at a Cadillac plant—and I thought I'd make some money and quit after a few months and go on to better things. I can recall walking into the factory one night and saying to the guy who was with me, "Little did Levine know that night as he passed through the portals to Detroit Transmission that one day all this would be his." I was transforming my life into a Horatio Alger fable, into a joke, knowing perfectly well this was impossible. In fact, I remember getting my first check from this factory, signed by the treasurer of General Motors. And he was the father of a girl I had gone to high school with. I went into shock. I thought, "No wonder I never got invited to those parties." I suddenly understood class perfectly.

I was playing the part of a factory worker. Later—at twenty-five—I *was* a factory worker, even though I'd finished college, and by this time I knew I was exploited, and I felt I was an idiot. I'd gone to college for this? I was badly married, I owed money, I was trapped in a life I despised, and unless poetry rescued me from the abyss, I was there for the duration. Then the girl I'd married and I parted, I worked for another year, saved money, and went off to Iowa. That's when my life became easier. I was twenty-six, and I'd learned how to live modestly: everything I owned—except for my typewriter—fit into one suitcase.

You've written that a turning point in your writing life was a dream you had about a factory you once worked in. "When I closed my eyes and looked back into the past," you wrote, "I did not see the blazing color of the forges of nightmare or the torn faces of the workers. . . . Instead, I was myself in the company of men and women of enormous sensitivity, delicacy, consideration. . . . In those terrible places designed to rob us of our bodies and spirits, we sustained each other." Could you talk about the people you worked with and your relationship with them?

It's hard enough for people to reach across the gulf of color or race, sex, age, what have you, without having to breach the gulf of the roar of machines. You had to get to know people in spite of the conditions.

I remember working at Cadillac with a young black guy from the South. Very young, maybe eighteen, a handsome, strong, cheerful fellow. We did things in tandem. One of us would take the stock off an overhead line and hand it to the other—we'd switch off—and the second guy would feed it into a machine and pass it on. The place was so dirty that we changed our clothes in a locker room before and after each shift. I remember one night dawdling in the locker room after work; it was midnight Friday, the workweek was over, and I probably didn't know where I wanted to go or what I wanted to do. I heard this odd noise coming from a toilet stall, and when the door opened there was this young fellow, the cheerful one. I asked him if he was okay, and he wondered why I asked. I said I knew it was his first week on the job, he was far from home, maybe it was tough. Right out he said, "I was crying. I'm lonesome. I don't know anyone, I hate this job." I said, "We all hate it, it's terrible work." In my mind I was saying, "Hang on, young fella," and he seemed to hear it. He put his hand on my shoulder. It was just a moment; I don't think that would happen at IBM. I don't think a man as big and handsome as he was, a man working in corporate America, would just unashamedly say, "I was crying."

I worked at a place called Brass Craft Manufacturing for a year. They made and chromed plumbing parts, and I was the person who mixed the chemicals for what were called the pickling tanks, where the parts were prepared for chroming. Each Monday, I cleaned out the tanks and made up a fresh soup. I rather enjoyed it, working on my own at my own sweet time. The rest of the week I hauled trays of copper tubing to the women who worked the polishing machines; they did the work that required quick hands. About half the women were black, half white, and most were up from the South; they had come for war work, but now that was gone and this was the best they could get. They were all older than I. They treated me like a kid brother. A few of them were beautiful, and I would have preferred another relationship, but you take what you get.

How did you get to know them?

We'd talk during our lunch break, which was all of twenty minutes. Sometimes they'd bring me things they'd baked, cake or cookies. Often we'd go to a bar at midnight after work and talk and share our stories. Some of them were mothers with children. They did not have easy lives, and yet they soldiered on. They had a wonderful ability to accept what they had and find joy in it, while I was very dissatisfied with my own life. I thought I should be writing my version of "Ode to a Nightingale." I was resentful of the factory work I had to do, partly because I saw it as something that was either going to delay my arrival into the kingdom of poetry or deny my entry. Little did I know it would become my subject matter.

Did any other of your coworkers make a particular impact on you?

The person who had the strongest impact was a man I met when I was very young, maybe fourteen or fifteen, a black man named Andy Griffith. I was his helper at a small grease shop, Automotive Supply Company. He must have been in his early forties when I first worked with him. He was up from

Alabama, had come for war work. He seldom talked about his personal life. He moved through the days with this amazing, quiet confidence. He didn't have any particular reason to be kind to me, but he was astonishingly considerate. I was supposed to be his helper, his assistant, but mainly he looked out for my welfare. He was always showing me how to do things. We worked on a truck together, delivering and picking up auto parts. I would go to pick something up, and he'd stop me. "No, Phil, you'll hurt your back that way," and then he'd show me how to do it. Sometimes we'd be hauling something together, and he'd see I wasn't up to managing my half, and he'd quietly signal me out of the way and do it by himself. He was enormously powerful, but he never made a display of his strength. Even though I didn't have a license, he taught me how to drive the truck, how to back it up through narrow channels. Once, at the Ford Rouge plant, we had to pick something up, and he actually drove the truck backwards while standing on the running board; later, he taught me how to do it. And he always worked at the same pace. If he was told to hurry, he'd just keep going at his pace. He made it clear to me I should set a pace at which I could work the whole day and just ignore what anyone said. You didn't cheat the boss or yourself.

He also was very well spoken, articulate, and very tactful. His lessons were like poems; they arrived clothed in the materials of the hour. For example, we were taking a lunch break on the back of the truck; he was smoking, and I went to light a cigarette of my own, and he stopped my hand and extended his cigarette and said, "Some day you may need that match." He was talking about a lot more than that match.

I saw him insulted once, his honesty questioned. He'd been working at this place for ten years or so, and he just quit in five minutes. You could not question his integrity.

When the Korean War broke out, in the summer of 1950, I was working on a road gang on U.S. 24; we worked twelve-hour days, six days a week, and I got to know the other men very well. Three of them stuck with me. One was a college guy like me, a philosopher, big, strong, wonderfully articulate. He was the first gay guy I got to know well, a man who just wanted to be left alone. I admired the way he just declared his sexuality, no apologies. Another guy was just out of prison for armed robbery: a little rat-faced guy about thirty who totally refused to do anything unless the boss was staring right at him. He told these terrific lies about his life as a gangster. The third guy was maybe sixty and should not have been doing this kind of work. Like Andy, he went at his own pace, but even his slow pace was too much for him, and one hot afternoon he had a mild heart attack. Cherry Dorn, white-haired, dignified and poor. He'd worked all his life, and what he had for it was a ruined body.

How did your coworkers react to your ambition to be a poet?

I was probably in my twenties before I shared my secret, and then no one looked askance. The only poet anyone seemed to know was Edgar Allan Poe. "Oh, you want to write 'The Raven.'" If they thought writing poetry was outrageous, they kept it to themselves. One guy I worked with for Railway Express—which was the UPS of the Stone Age—thought my hope to be a poet was marvelous. He was an unusual guy: big, handsome, rugged, an ex-sergeant in the infantry who'd fought in the Italian campaign and had gotten to Rome ahead of Mark Clark. He wasn't allowed to drive; I asked him why once, and he just said, "I'm a drunk." One autumn, we were working trunks, picking them up in Grosse Pointe, this wealthy suburb, for these kids who were going off to college. And he'd tell these kids, "My buddy here, Phil, should be going to Harvard; he's a genius poet, but he has to work this lousy job." The kids did not look impressed.

At the time, I was going to college part-time at Wayne University. This was during the McCarthy era, and I had to watch some of my professors disguise themselves as "patriots" and rat on their colleagues and students who they said were Communists, do anything to hang on to their tenured positions. I had this childish belief that people who lived with great literature would be inspired to noble behavior. That crashed fast. I don't think the people I worked with in the factories would have caved in to the House Un-American Activities Committee. It occurred to me that I might be lucky to be spending so much time with them.

Was there much labor unrest in the places you worked?

What I recall most vividly was a wildcat strike at Chevy. A guy had lost a hand to a huge punch press. Four men worked that machine: two fed the stock in on one side, and two others removed it after it had been stamped. Using tongs, they'd insert white-hot sheet metal into the press, pull their hands away, push this red button, and the press would come down. Apparently, the press came down without anyone pressing the button, and this fellow lost a hand. In an hour or two, the plant managers wanted the men to go back to work on the same press even though nothing significant had been done to repair the thing. It caused an instant strike. We all stopped working. These were not men with great skills or college educations who could walk away and find better jobs the next day. It certainly made most of my professors look small.

I remember a woman I once worked with; she completely broke down one night, just started to cry and curse, with tears streaming down her face. She was a very essential-looking person, all the excess cut away, with this strong jaw and olive skin, very striking. And usually she was very private, very withdrawn, and suddenly this outburst. We all stopped what we were doing, the noise stopped, and it was just her voice. This older woman asked her what was the matter. Finally, a sentence: "It's this god damned life, it's such shit." Everyone understood what she was saying. All those questions with intolerable answers—"What am I doing here?" "Will it ever get better?" "Can I keep going?"—had suddenly caught up with her. She was not an old woman by any means; she was probably younger than she looked. The women almost always looked older than they were—they had families, husbands, and these jobs. I've never forgotten that moment; it was a sort of communion in which all of us reached across the impossible gulfs that separated us. We were in this together.

How do you think the people you worked with retained their humanity in dehumanizing conditions?

I don't know that they did. When I was a freshman at Wayne, I got to know this wonderful guy, Jimmy Wilson. He'd been a great track star and running back in high school, and we were both in this boxing and wrestling class. The coach hated us. When I missed school because of Yom Kippur, he said, "It's not a holiday, it's a Jew-day." He would always pair off Jimmy and me against each other. Jimmy outweighed me by at least twenty-five pounds, and he could have bounced me around the room, but instead we faked these fights; we'd pretend we were hurting each other, and the coach would yell, "Kill him, kill him," and we'd break down and howl with glee.

About twenty years later, I was back in Detroit, sitting on a front porch, drinking a beer, and I saw this gray-haired, heavy-set guy with a lunch box under his arm coming down the street. It was Jimmy. He'd been such a joyous guy who took so much pleasure in his physical gifts and his intelligence, and although he was exactly my age he looked sixty-something. We talked for a few minutes; he'd never finished Wayne, he had a family, he worked at Dodge. Right then, I thought of Blake's Newton with all that heavy muscularity pulling him earthward.

It's not easy. I don't know the degree to which I survived, and I got out of that world at age twenty-six. It's made me suspicious, combative, angry, in ways I wish I weren't and can't shake. I feel it in my posture still, forty-five years later, a sort of "get out of my way" attitude. I see it in the way I deal with money or possessions. None of it is really mine; I can wake up tomorrow and it'll all be gone. What happens to people who are in that life until they're fifty or sixty? We internalize so much. It truly takes character to hang on to yourself when you're treated like crap, more character than I have. The poet Philip Larkin describes how a man shivers without shaking off the dread "that how we live measures our nature." I had to fight the terror of that realization all the time.

What do you think gave you the motivation, as a young man, to squeeze in time to write around your working hours?

The pure joy of writing poetry. It was the most thrilling thing I'd ever done. I doubt the poems were that good, but I felt myself growing stronger as a writer. I'd work all these hours, and then feel, I got it! Sometimes I felt transported: is this me? This guy who'd written the poem was so much smarter and more articulate than I. When you're writing well, you feel enormous—emotionally, spiritually, sometimes even physically—I'd never had such a glorious experience.

And when I wrote, I stopped being this insignificant little loser. I became a cousin to John Keats and Walt Whitman and Geoffrey Chaucer and Emily Dickinson. I joined the family of people who stuck at this poetry thing because there was nothing else to equal it. That's what kept me going.

Striking out from home without a glance back seems to be the American way—and yet your work reveals an enduring turning back; it's almost an immigrant sensibility. Could you comment on the value of keeping your eye on where you started and not solely on where you're going?

Always looking back is part of my nature. The common American notion of "off with the old, on with the new" has always offended me. The trophy wife thing, the move to the suburbs, the bobbed nose and the bobbed name—all that disgusts me. Maybe some of it comes from my pride in my family, my love for my parents and my grandfather, people who crossed a continent and an ocean with nothing and made lives for themselves in a strange land, at times a hostile one. I felt very grateful to my father and mother for being avid readers, for filling my childhood with books. Their intellectual curiosity, their struggles for freedom, their love of the arts; I was given a great heritage, one that defined who I was. In the way I've written I can see this loyalty to the past: my obsessions with Detroit, with working people, with the Spanish Civil War, with the look and feel of an America that's long vanished. I can see it in my life, too. There are loves I have that have carried me through my life, and they're such a great gift. The old lessons I got from my grandfather and Andy are still with me.

And poetry, too, has been faithful to me, and the poetry I inherited directed me toward the poetry that wasn't written. The very nature of being a poet, maybe any artist, is never to say, "Off with the old." It's to say, "Let me carry the old into the present and then into the future as best I can."

An Interview with Paul Mariani

Let's go back to the beginning. Tell us a little bit about your origins, your beginnings in Detroit.

I was born in 1928. My earliest memories are of being in a very strong familial setting: my father, my mother, my two brothers, living upstairs in the very house in which I was born on Pingree Avenue in Detroit, and my grandfather and grandmother living downstairs, my Aunt Belle nearby, still single. I'm unaware as a child of the tensions in the family. I'm unaware of the fact that we're living in a Catholic and not a Jewish neighborhood. I'm unaware of the fact that I'm Jewish. I'm just a kid growing up, and it isn't until I start school that my schoolmates remind me of my Jewishness. But the early memories are very warm, and there is a sense of family and a sense of containment.

Detroit was not the city it is now. It was a prosperous city. My grandfather and my father were partners in business. They were doing quite well. We were middle-class people. They had automobiles. My grandfather was the kind of guy who liked to dress well and look sharp, with pearl gray suits and hats, spats—a lady's man in spite of the fact that the ladies were taller than he was. Then I begin to sense things were not as sweet as they might be: troubles in the family.

Over what?

My Aunt Belle's first marriage was something of a disaster. You become aware at seven, eight, nine, of tensions in the family. Of course my father died when I was five.

What do you remember of your father?

A tall, slender, very affectionate man. I remember his tak-

From *Image*, "An Interview with Paul Mariani," (December 1995).

ing my twin brother and me out for automobile rides on week-end mornings. He traveled a lot so he was away quite a bit, but when he was home he liked to spend a lot of time with us.

Were your family members observant Jews?

By and large, no. Though quite often I went to *shul* with Zaydee, my grandfather. I rather enjoyed it, though I had no idea at first what was going on. A friend recently told me she'd gone to a Latin mass and was surprised by the length of it and the amount of standing and falling; only a few years ago this woman was a practicing Catholic. I told her what I liked best about the Orthodox Jewish shul were the visuals and the bou-quet, which was largely of tobacco and wine. The costuming was something, the beautiful, luxurious tallises. The Torah itself was stunning and handsomely robed. I liked the essen-tially impromptu nature of the service: men would just come in and pick up the chanting and walk around and exchange greetings, keep going at their own sweet pace, and leave when they'd done their thing. There would be conversations in Yid-dish but always in the same rhythm and with the same tonal qualities as the *dovening*. At the time I was hopeful of one day mastering these procedures, not, I think, to get closer to God. I had no notion of a God. I wanted entrance into this mysteri-ous world. It was the world of men. It wasn't until I began to study for my bar mitzvah that I got an idea of what the reli-gion was all about, but by this time—age ten to thirteen—I was far more enchanted by the greater American world.

Was there any political feeling in the neighborhood, especially, say, in the 1930s? The Spanish Civil War looms massively in your work. What did you hear in Detroit? What was the sense of that war?

By the time the war started, in 1936, I was eight. My mother was working full-time, and she had employed a woman in the summer to look after us. Florence Hickok was her name. She came from the Dakotas. She claimed to be related in some way to Wild Bill Hickok. She was like a political teacher to us. A real leftist. And she had a sharp sense of the significance of the war, that this was one of the struggles of democratic people against the rising ride of fascism.

She used the expression, "They're selling them down the river." The Spanish working people were being sold down the river the way American working people had been sold down the river by politicians; and the so-called democracies—France, Britain, the U.S.—were just looking the other way and letting Franco and the Nazis and the Italian Fascists have their way in Spain because they would rather crush a people's movement than see it triumph anywhere. She was right. After my father died, we weren't that well off financially, so we were living in much more of a working-class neighborhood. The kids I went to school with had brothers or cousins or uncles who'd gone off to Spain. So there was a sense that this was our war.

I was already aware of Hitler as an anti-Semite, and yet for reasons I've never figured out, my mother, my grandfather, my grandmother, and my aunt listened to radio broadcasts of Hitler, which would come over the airwaves translated. You could hear Hitler in the background and you'd get the translation. Also in Detroit there was this mad Catholic priest, Father Coughlin, who every Sunday preached pure Nazism about the monstrosity of the Jews and their international conspiracy. And you had Henry Ford publishing *The Protocols of Zion*. We were getting hit from all sides.

Ford: a name to conjure with. Many of your early jobs were auto related, weren't they, because of the Detroit auto industry?

Yeah. And my family was in an auto parts manufacturing business.

Weren't they using goons to put down labor unrest in the Detroit area, too? The Rouge River plant and all? At the time did you see a correlation between that kind of oppression and the kind of oppression going on in Europe?

Yes, absolutely. I was told as a kid that the huge German industrial empires were related to or controlled by the same people who controlled General Motors, Ford, and Chrysler. These captains of industry were leading a sort of conspiracy against ordinary workers. Henry Ford put a guy named Harry Bennett in charge of security. We knew a man who worked for Bennett, a painter. There was a horrible romantic painting of his in our house. This guy was a weekend painter; what he was full-time was an ex-con who had been paroled to Bennett to work as one of the goons and spies. They would go among the workers and listen for anti-Ford sentiment or people saying, "Let's unionize." There was no union at Ford at this time, not until the war.

Did Ford break all attempts at forming unions?

Yes. And finally there was "the Massacre at the Overpass." Walter Reuther and a guy named Dick Frankenstein and some of the other union leaders were badly beaten by goons with clubs and blackjacks. Fortunately this hideous event was caught by photographers from *Life* magazine, and the press Ford got was very bad. Though, by and large, the Detroit press was very conservative.

When did you begin writing poetry?

I can separate two clear careers which I've described in an essay in *The Bread of Time: Toward an Autobiography*. One is when I was in my early teens and I left my house and began to make compositions. Somewhere around the age of sixteen I stopped doing that. I don't exactly remember why. In school I was always being encouraged for my writing. Almost every teacher I had in grade school, in junior high, and high school just said, "You write like an angel. Why don't you think about becoming a writer?" Then in my junior year in high school I read Wilfred Owen, and I got really fascinated with poetry again. And that's when I started my second career.

What about Wilfred Owen attracted you?

I think he was the first semi-modernist poet—I can't call him a modernist—I read. He was as much of a modern poet as I was ready for at seventeen. This was during World War II, which I was waiting to become part of as soon as I finished high school. I was aware of a young man—Owen—addressing me from the point of view of a confidant, telling me what I deeply suspected was true: "You don't want this. And what you're hearing in the press and in the films, that's all lies. War is a nightmare that nobody should be involved in."

Here was a validation of my own suspicions about the nature of the Great War—of any war for that matter. I found him compelling and started again trying to write poetry. Shortly thereafter I entered Wayne University, and it was there at age eighteen that I began to read people like Hart Crane, Eliot, Auden, Steven Spender, and Wallace Stevens. I'd had no idea there was anything like this. That kind of stuff wasn't taught in the public schools back in the 1940s.

Did you have good teachers at Wayne University?

It was a mixed bag. The best teachers were superb. But I think that's probably true of almost any school. My first semester freshman year I got an awful woman, but my second semester I got a guy named Sinclair, who really encouraged me to become a writer and fostered in me a great deal of confidence about my writing. I had written a paper that was an anarchist diatribe on how I would like to see the world constructed. He told me, "Stay after class." He hadn't handed the paper back. I sat in the class and all the other students had gone. It was in one of these temporary, shabby buildings.

He said, "I don't agree with any of the ideas in this paper that you wrote, but the way you argue and the evidence you use and the writing itself: this is marvelous. I couldn't do as well. Even though I'm a much more conservative person politically and I'm a bit offended by your politics, the first time I read this I was swayed. I was ready to say you were right. You are an extraordinarily good writer." I said, "Really?" He said, "You're a much better writer than I am." I saw red pencil marks where he had corrected punctuation, and I said, "Look at all these." And he said, "They don't matter. That's what *I* get right. But I don't get this right," and he read me a couple of sentences. He said, "Those are marvelous sentences. Really."

You graduated from Wayne when?

1950.

Did you apply immediately for the University of Iowa?

No. I was doing factory work. After about a year I thought, "I'll get a master's degree in English." So I enrolled in Wayne in the master's program. It was slow going because I was working full-time. I was taking a course a semester. So I didn't go off to Iowa until 1953. I thought I had a grant there because in 1952 I applied but for a variety of reasons I didn't go. They had written back and said, "We'll give you free tuition and a certain stipend."

Did you continue to write poetry while you were working in the factories?

Yeah. Poetry and prose fiction.

Were you published yet?

I had tried once and was rejected.

And then Iowa in 1953. You enrolled for what? A three-year program?

No, I had no real intention of getting a degree. I went there in the belief that I had a fellowship, but when I got there, I didn't. I couldn't afford the out-of-state tuition, so I lied my way in. I got a room in Iowa City for ten or twelve bucks a month. Just a room, a small room, with no cooking privileges. Down the hall was a bathroom and a bathtub.

But Robert Lowell was there. I had been reading Lowell back in Detroit and thinking, "This is extraordinary." He was still a relatively young man. He would have been in his mid-thirties. It was Lowell's work that summoned me there.

You were lucky enough to have two of the premier poets in the American canon for teachers at Iowa. First Lowell and then John Berryman. I know you've written about this extensively, but what comes to mind in terms of what each man taught you?

I think the thing that Lowell taught me was that there was a softness in my work. That I might start a poem with something strong but I was writing more out of my ear than my brain or my experience, that I was a bit too hypnotized by the great musicians like Hart Crane and Dylan Thomas, and that I should really be reading a different poetry. The poet he urged on me was Thomas Hardy.

Yesterday I was in the New York Public Library and there was a display of manuscripts by fifty poets from John Donne to T. S. Eliot. Hardy is there, some of his manuscripts. And there's a little statement by Auden. It was just perfect; he said, and I'll paraphrase it: "My first model was Thomas Hardy. He was the perfect model for me, in the sense that he wasn't so eccentric that I couldn't follow him and not be myself. In fact, the further I went into Hardy the more I learned about myself, though when I imitated him too much, too carefully, too closely, I didn't write well. Somehow I was nearsighted or had astigmatism when I put on Thomas Hardy's spectacles." Hardy was very useful to me in the same way. Then I segued from Hardy to Frost. Frost was a very useful encounter because he had a formal rigor that I had to become aware of. So the kind of easy self-indulgence that I was practicing—which was really out of bad Dylan Thomas, not good Dylan Thomas—began to vanish from my work, I hope.

Berryman was a whole different kettle of fish, in the sense that I don't think Lowell ever took me that seriously. I'm not sure he took any of his students very seriously. He was a man on the brink of a terrible breakdown. It was probably very difficult for him to focus his extraordinary sensibility on us. One thing I left out of my essay in *The Bread of Time* was that personally I think Lowell was a very kind man. I wish I'd gotten that into the essay. While I was at Iowa I had an accident. I was hit by a car. I wasn't terribly injured but I had a slight concussion from a fall I took after being hit. First my glasses were broken and I had to go get new ones, and the other thing was that it took me a couple of days to focus my eyes. And I'm walking down the street and suddenly there's a man who taps me on the shoulder and says, "Are you okay, Phil?" I turned and focused my eyes as well as I could and it was Lowell. He said, "What happened to you?" He was very concerned. "Are you okay? Can I give you a ride? Do you need to go somewhere?" I suddenly saw there was a good-hearted man here. Though in class he seemed cold and aloof, there really was a warm man living inside Robert Lowell. I'll never forget that. There wasn't anything he could do for me, but when I told him my glasses were broken, he actually offered me money to get new glasses. He let me know he was there and that I could count on him. I'm sorry I left that out of *The Bread of Time.*

Anyway, Berryman came in as professor. And for Berryman the class was like thirteen people that in a way he had to charm, that he had to exhort, rouse. He saw it as an enormous challenge. My sense was that for Lowell teaching was a way of making a living. For Berryman it was a kind of emotional enterprise, an almost spiritual enterprise: can I raise these people up to be the poets they're capable of being? What he— like Lowell—taught me more than anything else was that I should stop loitering in my own poems. "Don't waste these lines. Don't fill in material. If it's no good, cut it out. You don't have an allegiance to the form of a sonnet; you have an allegiance to making a passage of power and beauty. And form will serve you. Keep trying. Write everything." Also, Berryman loved the idea that I was bringing the anger of American working people into my poetry. He just loved that, though I doubt he ever lifted anything heavier than a pen or a check. He also loved Jewish humor in poetry.

When can you first point to a recognizable Levine style?

I think in looking back on it that nothing I wrote that year at Iowa or in the long summer after that year when I went back to Detroit and worked really would matter to me now. But then, at the end of the summer of 1954, I went to North Carolina and married Franny. And I stopped working. She worked. During the following year when we lived in Tallahassee, Florida, I worked on poetry like I'd never worked on it. You know, four or five hours a day writing a lot and reading everything I could get my hands on. I went down to Tallahassee and finished my master's degree at Wayne; I wrote a thesis on Keats's "Ode on Indolence." The first poem I ever published was in the spring issue of the *Antioch Review* in 1955. And suddenly a lot of magazines were taking my poetry.

That early voice is a more formal voice in many ways, or at least it has a more formal finish.

Yes, that is, it's rhymed poetry, it's metrical poetry, it's frequently pentameter, but it's also trimeter and tetrameter. Occasionally I'd even venture into a longer line to get a sort of galloping or looser thing. But by and large I would rhyme. I felt constrained to rhyme.

Why?

Well, my life was in some ways chancy and disordered. I mean here you are, you're a poet and you've got a BA in English. You've got a wonderful wife who's working as a costumer in a university theater at Florida State. You have no idea where the future is going to take you. You know that even if you finish this master's degree, the phone is not going to ring and the University of Michigan is not going to say, "Hey, we need you. We've got to have you as a teacher. You're great." I didn't know what the hell was going to happen. So with all of this life whirring around me, it was nice to sit down and add some form to that life through the use of formal structures in poetry.

When you're working in formal poetry, also, there is a way in which you see your progress. You really can see it and feel it. You feel your growing ease with tercets or sonnets or just stanza forms or blank verse or whatever it is you're working with. You feel a growing sense of mastery. Also, I was reading stuff from every era in English poetry and feeling that I was learning things about the way Dryden and Wyatt and Pope and Wordsworth and Milton handled the line, the way Milton and Wordsworth handled whole passages, using rhyme and yet getting the kind of sweep that you get in blank verse.

I began seeing Dylan Thomas and Lowell from another point of view. Here were these old heroes and I was seeing that these were guys heavily immersed in a long and wonderful tradition. Even though I was living in utter isolation—I didn't know a single person writing poetry in Tallahassee—I did have a family of poets. They stretched from Wyatt through Wallace Stevens, and here I was, doing the same zany thing.

William Carlos Williams also began to assert himself for me. I don't remember when I first started reading Williams with that kind of seriousness. Probably back at Wayne. One of the things that got me reading him seriously again was Randall Jarrell's essay in *Poetry and the Age*. Yeats was another powerful influence. I loved how he could control the poetry and the sweep of poetry. And also the way he could talk about very personal things as though they were of momentous historical importance, about his friends and his enemies. I thought, "Well, Christ, if he can do that for Dublin early in the century maybe I can do it for Detroit later in the century." That was a very inspiring and hopeful thing that I got from Yeats. But in Williams I suddenly said to myself—I was reading Whitman too—"Hey Levine, you're also an American. Don't forget it." I saw in Williams and Whitman two poets who politically were much more akin to me because of my vision of what an American ought to be than, say, poets like Yeats or Stevens, whom I admired enormously.

When did your shift to free verse begin?

In 1957 I went out to Stanford on a writing fellowship and

worked with Yvor Winters. I think that's when it started to happen. His insistence that writing in form is somehow a moral act struck me as inane, and I watched his copycat students echoing this idea and it got more inane. On the other hand, I think he was a wonderful teacher if you rebelled against him, because he was so knowledgeable. He was utterly convincing. It was like meeting the great rabbi and you say, "What do I do with my life?" "Ah, son, I will tell you what to do with your life. You will go out and you will do X, Y, and Z and then you will be a good man and you will go to heaven." And that was sort of what Winters did, you know: "Ah, sons, you will write in the manner of Fulke Greville about the heart, the truth, the soul, etc., and you'll do it in rhyme and meter and you'll be a good person, etc., etc. Right reason will dominate over those terrible surgings of the unconscious and the id. And don't fuck too much either or you'll go to hell."

He once told me Donne was oversexed. And I said, "Is such a thing possible?" "Don't be funny, young man!" he said. I said, "Where did you get this evidence? How do you know what Donne was?" And he said something like, "He had nine children." So I said, "What does that prove? That he was either lucky or unlucky nine times?" "Don't be disrespectful, boy!" So there was a kind of silliness there. At the same time, there was a very high seriousness. And I liked him. I found him a curmudgeon and a difficult man, but also, I saw in him something of the same thing I saw in Lowell: that hiding in there and not wanting people to see it was a very tenderhearted man, a very frustrated but loving man, who didn't know how to act out his affections and yet felt them powerfully. And he was very kind to me. So I enjoyed working with him, but I think partly as an act of rebellion I felt the need to defy him, to write à la Williams.

The marriage of the colloquial with the lyrical was and still is important for you. Does that concern come out of William Carlos Williams?

The concern and marriage were always there—it was my language. But when you write ten years or so in traditional meters that's always going to be with you. Basically the poetry I was reading was in formal meter. I was still loving Hardy and

Crane and Wordsworth and Keats. I was still reading all these formal poets. At the same time I was trying to wed the lyric and the conversational. So I'm always sort of trying to get some lyrical underpinning. I don't want my poems to sound like chat. At the same time, I don't want the diction to be false or elevated the way it often becomes in bad formal poetry.

What's the earliest poem you wrote that you feel is distinctively your own?

A poem in my first book *On the Edge* [Stone Wall Press, 1963] called "Small Game." I don't think it's in my *New Selected Poems*. It's about hunting. I think it's the first poem in which I'm able to combine the lyric with a sense of freedom. It's in rhymed syllabics ["In borrowed boots which don't fit / and an old olive greatcoat, / I hunt the corn-fed rabbit, / game fowl, squirrel, starved bobcat"] It has a sense of mystery to it. I wrote it while I was at Stanford. There are a few boo-boos, things I didn't get right.

Probably the next poem that I wrote about which I still would say, "Yes, that was an important poem," was "On the Edge," a short metrical poem. I think it has voice, humor, a direct encounter with experience, and a considerable amount of anger. I wasn't dealing with the industrial experience yet. I tried very hard over these years to write poems about my life in Detroit and working in a factory and also about my family, but it seemed to me that none of those poems was any good.

What was missing so that you couldn't do what you wanted to yet? What did you need before you could believe in what you were writing about the industrial experience and about your own family?

I think what I needed had nothing to do with technique. It had everything to do with the way I was going to see my experience. Technically I think I was capable. But emotionally or spiritually I was still too close to the experiences or too young or they were still too raw for me. I had to come to terms with them emotionally. When I wrote about the industrial experience, which I did quite often, the poems tended to turn into a rant. The poems were melodramatic because the experience itself was so extraordinary and humbling. You disappeared as a person in those places.

So I had to come to some point where I would say, "Stop

focusing on the fact that you were miserable and exhausted and underpaid and exploited. And start focusing on the fact that you were in the company of extraordinary people and they accepted you and you grew as a person." It took me a while to see that that was also what my experience was. I don't know how I came to that. But suddenly I began writing about it in that way.

Do you have a favorite poem of yours about Detroit and about working people, one that you particularly like?

Yeah, I like the poem "A Walk with Tom Jefferson." It grew out of a particular experience. I was teaching at Tufts University at the time and got an invitation to come back to Wayne University, now Wayne State, to speak and read some poems at a retirement party for my old teacher Jay McCormick, a fiction writer and a lovely man. I said I would do it and it was supposed to be a surprise. He didn't know I was coming. Of course Wayne State said, "We don't have much of a budget but we'll pay your airfare, etc. Just fly in, tell us when, and we'll be there. We'll handle everything." Well, I arrived at the Detroit Metropolitan Airport and there's a woman with a sign that says "Philip Levine." "Ah," I think, "There's the woman who's going to drive me to Detroit." No, she works for Northwest Airlines and she hands me an envelope. I open it up. It's instructions on how to take the bus into Detroit. I thought, "Ah, Wayne is doing it again." I was supposed to read at three in the afternoon. I thought, "You jerks, I'm going to get even with you. I'm going to show up exactly at the moment I'm supposed to read. I'm going to make you people think I'm not here."

So I took the bus in and began walking around Detroit. I walked over to the ballpark area, looked at things and met people and talked to people, and that's the genesis of the poem. That day was like a gift, or what do they say in New Orleans?—a *lagniappe*. I didn't *know* it was a gift at the time, but I was feeling generous in my heart toward my old teacher, remembering. And then I went to the event, I did the thing, and I went back to Somerville, Massachusetts, where I was living, and within a very short time I embarked on this poem. The finished poem is only about 650 lines, but the first morning that I started writing, I probably wrote 900 lines.

In one day?

Maybe two. I mean I worked the whole day. It was just coming. It changed forms. I started with one form, I changed to another. I just kept working and I worked into the second day and then I looked at it, typed everything up, and realized that at a certain point it went dead. I'd introduced too many characters. I had myself in the poem as a guy walking through the city, especially through this one neighborhood. And I had this guy Tom Jefferson that he encounters, and then I introduced some other people. And they weren't working. I cut those 900 lines down finally to about 300 lines that I was happy with. The poem sat there in that form for over a year and a half, unfinished.

One day I reread it and asked myself, "What's lacking here?" And I thought, I don't get enough of Tom." Then it occurred to me I'd left out part of what happened to me that day. Part of what happened to me was that finally, about twenty minutes before I was supposed to appear at the party and read, I suddenly looked at my watch. I'd been so absorbed in talking to people in this neighborhood where they were going into this preindustrial era and farming and growing vegetables and raising animals—but I suddenly saw what time it was. I had to take a taxi to get to the art museum where the party was being held. So I hailed a cab, and the guy pulled over—a black man, probably about forty years of age. I told him exactly where I wanted to go, a particular door in the museum. And he said, "You must know this city." I said, "Yeah, I used to live here." He said, "Yeah, you *left* us, didn't you?" And I said, "Yeah." He said, "Well, all the smart people left." And he said, "What're you doing?" and I described what I'd come back for—that I was a poet and I'd come back for the retirement party.

He said, "Are you going to make him laugh or are you going to make him cry—your old buddy?" I said, "I hadn't thought about it. But now I'm going to try to do both." Then he said, "Oh man, that's biblical." I didn't know what he meant by that. What is he saying? Am I hearing born-again talk? So I said to him, "What do you mean by 'that's biblical'?" He pulled the cab over to the side of the street and he said, "You know, you and I could become friends. You know that? If we knew each other well, I think we could become friends. Let's say we did." I said, "Yeah."

"And here we are," he began. "What's your favorite drink—alcohol, you know?" I said, "Irish whisky." "Okay, mine's bourbon. Now you see that bar over there? Let's say that you and I would meet frequently at that bar, we'd have a drink and talk, and then one day you're in the cab here and I'm taking you someplace, but instead of getting out on the curbside, before I can say anything to you, you get out on the street side and—wham—you're dead. Well, today is September 23. Every September 23, I'd park the cab here, I'd walk up to that bar, I'd order two drinks, my bourbon and your Irish whisky, I'd drink mine for me and yours for you. That's biblical." The guy was great. Then he took me to where I had to get out. We parted, and I never saw him again.

But it was that phrase he used, the language and the emotion that he had. I said, "That's missing from the poem. I've gotta get that, that largeness of spirit that this guy had. I gotta get that into the character Tom." And I wrote the second half of the poem in one day: 300-and-some lines. Then I refined it a bit, but basically I wrote it in one day. I could go right to the point and show you where I stopped the first time, the place where I'm describing the ballpark at night, and all the people are shouting. That's where I stopped, and then I took off at that point and picked up a refrain line and kept going to the end.

Let's talk for a moment about the pervasive Spanish influence in your work. When did that enter into your poetry? Could you talk a bit about your two trips to Spain in the 1960s and what they've meant to you?

We went first in 1965; it was in some ways a very difficult year because we were poor. On the other hand, it was one of the most memorable and valuable years of my life. The good side of being poor was that it brought us so close together as a family, it made us dependent on each other in ways we hadn't been. I got to know my kids in ways I hadn't known them. We had no TV, we saw only one film during that year. I became the storyteller of the house. We had to entertain ourselves.

Gradually I began to meet people. First Hardie St. Martin, who was then doing a huge anthology of modern Spanish poetry translated by American poets. He enlisted my help. I got a wonderful Catalan poet to become my Spanish teacher, and I helped him with his English. The novelist John A. Williams moved into our village. Then the great fiction writer Henry Roth came over to Spain, where they made a film about him for PBS. Then I met Tom McGrath in a bar in Barcelona, and he settled in our village, which was only six or seven miles from the center of Barcelona, fifteen minutes by car, maybe less by train. Tom settled near us for a time. Then I met Bob Coover who was living down the way in Tarragona, about an hour south, with his wife and two daughters. It was a very exciting time for me. After I got some Spanish I began doing my first translations, which Hardie properly tore to shreds. The poetry was exploding in my head. All I'd known of Spanish poetry were the translations of García Lorca. Suddenly I was struggling with Machado, Miguel Hernández, Miguel de Unamuno, Rafael Alberti, Jorge Guillén. Not having to teach, I discovered I had more energy to write than I'd ever thought I'd had. I'd been teaching four courses a semester in Fresno.

Why did you decide to translate? Was there something in the voice of these poets that you wanted to bring over into your own voice? Was there a foreignness there, something that made you reach?

In some respects, translating a poem is almost like writing a poem. You read the poem in the original and you say, "If I can carry just a portion of this into English, isn't this going to be marvelous?" So then you struggle with it, the way you do writing poems of your own. And a good many times you fail, just like writing a poem of your own. Occasionally you succeed and you carry that essential lyric structure as well as the emotional content into the translation. The first principle in translating, it seems to me, is to make Pablo Neruda or whomever you're translating sound in English almost as articulate as he does in the original. The worst thing you can do is take a poet who's gorgeous in the original and make him a stumblebum in your own language.

In your poetry I find not so much a religious but a spiritual dimension, at moments almost a mystical experience, a way of seeing things the way God or one of Rilke's angels might see them: someone above and removed from the experience itself, looking down upon the human dimension. Do you feel this in your poetry?

No, I don't think I'm seeing things the way an angel or a god might see them. I'm delighted that you find a spiritual dimension, but in truth I never planned to achieve that; I wouldn't know how. What I am aware of is that in my imagination scenes from the past, people, events have taken on a sort of glow and a patina as though I plucked them out of a great painting, as though the light were not the light of Detroit falling through the broken skylight of Detroit Transmission on September 7, 1948, but rather the light of Caravaggio hitting this face and highlighting that hand. My memory seems to have turned some of these old moments into Italian art.

When I go back in memory to these events I see them in a timeless light that accentuates what needs to be accentuated. Perhaps I get some of that quality into the poems, perhaps that's what you're seeing. I don't think I can say much more because I haven't planned it. If my people, Cipriano Mera and Tom Jefferson, acquire the significance of saints and heroes, well, that's wonderful. They *are* my saints and heroes.

There is no tradition from the Bible or elsewhere out of which you're coming that would explain this?

Perhaps 1st and 2nd Samuel, *The Iliad, King Lear, War and Peace.* All those great Italian and Flemish paintings I've stared at. They all did it better than I—that is, captured what they remembered or imagined or saw. Of course I've only given you the classy influences; I should add the 1930s movies I thought I couldn't live without, the daytime radio serials I cast and dramatized in my head, the look of Jake LaMotta and Laurent Dauthuille in the overhead lights the night they fought in Detroit for the middleweight title. Sandy Saddler and Willy Pep fighting in Yankee stadium a couple years later. A guy coming into a drug store at Livernois and Davison [in Detroit] with blood streaming from his shoulder and dripping off his fingers, a guy needing help. I was a child struck dumb. The sources are life.

A good part of your poetry is concerned with the suffering of working people. Can poetry offer any consolation for that suffering, or some deeper insight into the meaning of suffering, if suffering indeed has meaning?

Poetry can offer anything it's pleased to offer; I don't know how many people will derive consolation from it. *I* have felt its consoling power. Keats's great letter on the Vale of Soul Making has done as much as anything to explain to me the meaning and use of suffering. But a lot of the poetry I love isn't interested in consoling anyone for anything.

What do you think of the formulation that at some level all poets are in search of a redemptive vision, a way of reconfiguring or lifting human experience so that we can see its inherent dignity and worth?

What we have in fact are all these poets using different languages—with their various riches and limitations—for an enormous variety of reasons and to achieve an enormous variety of ends. Among us have been the poets of redemptive vision, bless their concern. I'm sure for some readers it works. I did not feel after reading *Paradise Lost* that the ways of God to man were justified. I did feel I'd read an amazing poem full of fire and doubt; I'd lived with language used with extraordinary power and originality. I probably saw the world differently just as I did after living with Dante's vision or at least the portion I grasped. Still, I wasn't in the least tempted to become a Christian, not even a tapestry Catholic, one converted by the beauties of the Catholic artistic heritage and liturgy. I can't imagine the poet today who could actually believe as he sat down to write that his or her reader was going to have an easier time dealing with injustice and loss after reading what was about to be written. That seems like a plan for disaster.

Can a viable religious poetry be written in our time?

Of course it can. And it is being written. Czeslaw Milosz is certainly a religious poet. What else can we call his poems that struggle with the meaning of Christian faith in a century during which people who call themselves Christian carry out barbaric acts not to be believed? What else can we call his struggles with the meaning of being, of love, of the separate self, of history? Gary Snyder is a religious poet. The question "What are my duties to the earth and the living things of the earth?" is a religious question.

Lowell's early poetry was not only religious; it was Christian, whatever that may mean. Perhaps it was actually Hebrew. "The Quaker Graveyard in Nantucket" is an homage to the power and majesty of the God of the Old Testament, though he does let "Our Lady of Walsingham" have two stanzas. The poem has something of the grandeur and magic of those poems in the Book of Job. Today religious poetry may not be that fashionable, but the good poets never care about fashion. I see the young writing religious poetry. Some of the recent work of Mark Jarman is not only overtly religious; it's terrific. Same goes for the work of Dennis Sampson. I find much of the work of Jane Kenyon religious as well as extraordinary. I've largely skipped over my own generation: Merwin, Stern, Ginsberg. And what of Charles Wright, who today is writing the most beautiful poetry in the world?

What are the particular challenges for a poet who wishes to confront the mystery of God's presence or absence in our lives?

The challenges? The first is probably not to sound pompous. I think it would be a mistake to regard oneself as The Poet Dealing with God's Presence. Or His Absence. God is absent from García Lorca's New York City. He was murdered along with all the ducks and cows and hogs and pigeons slaughtered "to accommodate the tastes of the dying." But of course García Lorca doesn't belabor that. He turns his attention to the cat squashed in the street and the janitors assigned to the little hells of their lives and the button counters who "drift in office numbers." Certainly another challenge is not to sound like Billy Graham or Cardinal O'Connor.

The deepest challenge may be to discover your actual feelings and to state them without grandiosity or self-pity or self-importance. I tried it once in a poem entitled "To My God in His Sickness." Galway Kinnell did it magnificently in his Avenue C poem ["The Avenue Bearing the Initial of Christ into the New World"]. Not a false move, every line rings true. *The* challenge no matter what your theme or obsession is to write with originality, truth, grace, and liveliness, to make words delighted to be among each other. That may sound easy, but I've spent over fifty years trying to get it right, and I'm still learning.

An Interview with Wen Stephenson

You're almost exactly the same age as the Beat poets Allen Ginsberg and Gary Snyder. Have you ever felt part of a generation?

Yes, I have. There was a period in my life, during the Vietnam War, when I felt very proud to be in the generation I'm of. We put away our petty divisions and labels and became coworkers, you might say, in the struggle against the war. I was reading with Ginsberg and Snyder—and with Robert Bly and Galway Kinnell and W. S. Merwin and Adrienne Rich—at various events. The first public readings I ever gave were in San Francisco with Gary Snyder in 1958.

What do you think of generations, schools, and movements?

I have mixed feelings. When I was at Stanford in the late 1950s I got to know the British poet Thom Gunn, who was associated with "The Movement"—which included other British poets like Philip Larkin and Kingsley Amis. But they had nothing in common other than a reaction against the mysticism and the high seriousness that you got in Dylan Thomas and George Barker during and just before World War II. I asked Gunn, "How do you feel about being labeled as a Movement poet?" and he said, "Well, it got me in the anthology."

I see that labeling schools and movements is a convenience for critics and readers, but when I look at, say, Ginsberg and Snyder—two poets I really love—I don't see that they have a hell of a lot in common.

Maybe a certain spirituality . . .

Yeah, you're right—the influence of Eastern religion.

But that doesn't have much to do with style.

From *Atlantic Unbound*, "An Interview with Wen Stephenson" (April 1999).

No, they're very different. Allen comes so directly out of Whitman, and Gary comes so directly out of Asian poetry and Kenneth Rexroth. There's such an attention to natural detail and quiet movement in Snyder's work, and there's such marvelous rhetoric and bombast in Ginsberg's best work—and also an enormous play of wit that you don't find in Snyder. I think they're both marvelous poets.

There's been such an emphasis recently on reading poetry aloud. Listening to some of the old recordings of modernist poets—I guess some of the earliest recordings we have of poets reading—they sound so markedly different from how people read today. Was there a moment when people started reading differently? Was it the Beats in the 1950s?

No. Here in America it was one poet—one poet changed everything. And curiously enough it was an English poet: Dylan Thomas. He came to the States and read with a fluency and ease and drama and power that nobody on the American scene commanded. I mean, William Carlos Williams was a terrible reader, for example. Wallace Stevens was pretty good, but he kind of droned on. e. e. cummings was a good reader. Edna St. Vincent Millay sounded hysterical—as though her foot were in the oven and she were calling for the fire department. Mostly the readings were overly dramatic or hyperbolic—or else they were just boring. When I heard W. H. Auden I hardly knew what he was saying. He was such a terrible reader—and he was drunk . . .

Did you ever hear Pound read?

Only on records. Oh, very dramatic, with that screwball accent he had.

Do you think there's a relationship between the way poets were reading and the way they wrote? Did Dylan Thomas actually influence people that way?

Thomas had an incredible impact on American poetry. If you were to go back and look at *Poetry* magazine in the 1950s—when he was here in the States making money by giving readings—you would discover that urban poets who had been writing about things like racism and smog and overcrowding, and writing socialist poems were suddenly out watching owls. Off in the distance are hay rakes, and farmers are burning the husks from last year, and planting season is coming—I mean, these poems are coming right out of Manhattan! They invented a whole landscape—and then they stopped. Thomas died, and everybody went back to what they were doing before.

I heard Thomas read several times and was hypnotized by him. But I was very young at the time, and I realized that in order to write like that there was a lot I was going to have to learn to be able to control the line so beautifully and to get that resonance that he had in his writing. And, of course, a lot of his poems are terrible. He could read the phonebook and make it sound terrific. At the end of his career he was largely just imitating himself, which was sad to see.

You touch on a good point: the difference between performance and actually writing poetry.

I don't think that performance has helped American poetry. I really don't. I think a number of American poets have almost ruined their careers by going out and getting that kind of attention—going from campus to campus and being sort of awe inspiring for an hour and a half and feeding on the adulation. The process of writing poetry depends on being alone in a room, and being comfortable being alone for long periods of time—almost reveling in solitude and slow time. I've had friends tell me, younger poets, that when they came back from their early reading tours they'd get very depressed. I guess they were waiting for applause as they picked up pen and paper. But there is no applause.

Your new collection, The Mercy, *is dedicated to the memory of your mother, who just died this past year, at age ninety-four. Your parents and their experience loom large in your poetry—as do your grandparents, your extended family. In the collection's opening poem, "Smoke," you speak of "the mythology of a family." What do you think about the idea that your work is a kind of "mythology" of an American family's experience?*

When I speak of "the mythology" in that poem, I really mean a way of losing someone. It's something I've observed even with my own children—they mythologize me, and in a sense they get it all wrong. I'm sure this is what I've done with my whole family: I've seized on certain things and raised them to the level of truth, whether they're true or not, and in focusing on these things I have, in a way, lost a good deal of the complexity of the living person.

You mention my "extended family." A lot of those people in my poems never existed. For example, sisters walk in and out of my poems, but I don't have any sisters. I used to say to my students, "Why be yourself if you can be somebody interesting? Imagine a life. Imagine yourself being something other than what you are."

In much of your work there's a recurring specificity of time (days, months, years) and of place—"this was Michigan in 1928," to use one example. And yet many of your poems seem to inhabit the past, present, and future all at once. Can you comment on this?

It's something that I started to do in my late forties and early fifties, and I think the reason was that I came to an awareness that in my most inspired moments I was actually living in all three times. That is, I was obviously in the present, but there was a way in which I brought with me the reality of the past and was in some ways trying to project it into the future, almost give it breath so that it went into the future. There were times when I really felt as though I were living in all three time "zones." I wanted to capture that quality—a personal sense of being that I've found enormously thrilling.

The first time I captured it in a poem I can remember thinking, Well, that's what I wanted to capture. "New Season," it's called, in *The Names of the Lost*. It's a poem about the future and my son, and the past and my mother, and the present and myself. It's something I've tried to do since—but not overdo. I think the poem "Salt and Oil," in *The Mercy*, is a poem like this. I think it's my favorite in that book.

What does your way of bringing narrative and lyric poetry together say about the relationship between history and autobiography?

I've always had a sense that history was far too selective, that a great many people—which would include just about everybody I know—have been deemed unsuitable subjects for history. I began as a fiction writer, and I had a real impulse toward narrative, toward storytelling. Then I saw in Yeats a capacity to merge extraordinary music, as in "Easter 1916," with the telling of a story. And I saw it in Hardy's poems, too. Beautiful. Hardy's such a storyteller. Yeats and Hardy are two very early influences on me—really powerful influences. So, I thought, what if I use the vocabulary (and to some degree the movement) of William Carlos Williams but also swipe from Hardy and Yeats, and from Dylan Thomas, who was another great influence, and make a somewhat more sonorous poem? To unite those elements and then tell these stories that others weren't telling—I guess that was my strongest impulse. I just wanted to tell the stories of people whom I found extraordinary and dear. I saw them pass from the world, and nobody said a goddamn word about them, so I said, "Well, this is a subject matter that is mine and mine alone."

You have a tendency in many of your poems to pause and inject a statement addressed directly to the reader, as though you're stepping out from behind the curtain. It's almost as though you're saying, "Look, I'm not going to bullshit you"—or, "maybe I've been bullshitting you up to now, but . . ." What's going on at these moments?

It's a technique, or a device, that I've found only partly fulfilled in W. H. Auden's early poems. He was a great love of mine when I was in my twenties and early thirties. I still love those poems. There's a way in which they're very strategic poems. They seem to understand that if you're going to say something difficult or hard about the nature of our experience, the reader will resist, and so you have to involve the reader shrewdly.

It's my sense that the reader is so often a suburban person. I published a lot of my poems in the *New Yorker* for many years, and I got the idea that my readers were really suburbanites who maybe on the train pick up the magazine, thinking, I wonder what I'm going to get for dinner tonight—and then they see this poem. I recognize that these are the hardest people to get to—they're deeply protected, they've survived in the zoo of New York, and they're not going to let a goddamn poem upset their equanimity. What I saw in Auden was a shrewd way of getting to you, surprising you, getting you off balance. You're right about the fact that I like to construct what I hope are beautiful fabrics and then suddenly enter in and say, "Wait a minute"—catch readers off balance, entangle them. I really think that's what Auden was doing: entangling us in the cloth of his poem, sort of confusing us, and then trying as best he could to make us spin out of it in some way and see the truth—or what he thought was the truth.

I think the first time I used this well enough to entangle readers was in *What Work Is,* in a poem called "Coming Close." So I said, "Shit, I'll try that again." And I have, and you've noticed it. I guess I'm getting to the point where I'd better stop. Because if I start doing it too much it'll become a tick.

Fair enough. But the way you've used it so far, I think, is extremely effective. It seems to reveal something about your personality. It's likable.

Well, thank you. I enjoy doing it. There's another aspect, too. As you age you begin to build up levels of nonsense between you and the past. You used the term *mythologize* before—to me, mythologizing is really a subtle way of lying. But you're only being dishonest to yourself. You construct a kind of history, a fabric, that in a way protects you from the past and its harsher, more difficult moments. A lot of this technique has to do with constructing one truth and then wiping it away with a second one. It's the process of writing: you start with a truth, and you break through to a deeper one.

There are a number of poems in the new collection in which you lament the failure of words to capture experience and do justice to memory. Have your feelings about the efficacy of language, and by extension poetry, changed over time?

Oh, they've changed enormously. Originally, my vision was for *The Mercy* to be a book about language. That wasn't going to be the open theme of it, but it was going to be the true subtext—the failure of language, or the various successes and failures of language. And, in fact, I had picked out a title poem that is no longer in the book—a poem called "On the Language of Dust," which I published years and years ago. As it turns out, the book now has more to do with journeys—from innocence to experience, and youth to age, and clarity to confusion and back again, and life to death, etc.—and "The Mercy" is the central poem. A lot of poems that are obsessed with language didn't make it into the book. They'll go in another book, or they'll just swim out into the sea . . .

To be truthful, when I began writing poetry I thought language could do anything. And I thought I could do anything with language. I'm talking about a guy who's twenty years old, saying, "I'll master this crap, and I'll do anything that's necessary." But as I got older, I began to realize, both in daily living and in what I read and what I wrote, that I was often coming up against the limits of my ability to use language, or my ability to comprehend language.

I also became more and more aware of how much idle chatter went on in the world. It seemed to me there was so much prattling and that the world was full of meaningless words. In my second book, there's a poem called "Silent in America" (written around 1966) that was built around the fact that I was mugged once, and I got a broken jaw, and I couldn't talk because my jaw was wired together. I spent two months listening. I just listened to everybody: my children, my friends, my wife, my brother. They were boring the hell out of me! I became aware of how language was being used—usually not to communicate but to disguise, to obfuscate. It was only two months of my life, but it was a powerful experience.

There's a poem in the new book—"'He Would Never Use One Word Where None Would Do'"—that gets its title from a quotation from the wife of a famous jazz saxophonist named Frankie Trumbauer, who played with Bix Beiderbecke. After he died his wife was interviewed about her life with Frankie, and that's what she said—it was very nice living with him, but he almost never said anything. And I was just so thunderstruck by it. I read it at exactly the time that my wife was very sick, in the hospital in New York, and a friend of mine, knowing I needed some kind of comfort, spent a lot of time with me. He's a very laconic kind of guy, and he hardly ever said anything. (He's the guy in the poem.) But he was an enormous comfort, without saying anything. I could just feel his presence so powerfully and his hopes for her recovery and my better spirits. It was so touching, and I thought, There are some things that don't require language and in fact can almost be ruined by language.

There's a great irony in all of this, of course . . .

That's what I live by.

In your essay "The Poet in New York in Detroit," in The Bread of

Time, *you write about the influence of Keats and of the Spanish poet Federico García Lorca. You give Lorca credit for enabling you to write a poem like "They Feed They Lion," a response to the Detroit riots of 1967. How has politics informed your poetry over the years? Have you ever found it difficult to reconcile poetic beauty and ugly political truth?*

No. Let's put it this way: I think that in twentieth-century poetry the beauty is found in the fullness of the expression, and the degree to which the poet is able to capture, through detail and rhythm, a particular scene—for example, in a poem like Robert Lowell's "The Mouth of the Hudson," a beautiful little poem about a hideous landscape. Or, say, in Hart Crane's "Repose of Rivers"—he also has a river, the Mississippi, running into the sea in this gorgeous ecstatic moment when the river loses its identity by becoming one with the gulf. They're marvelous scenes, but what makes them marvelous is the degree to which they're captured and not what the actual condition of the world was that inspired those poems.

As for Keats, I think he inherited an aesthetic that only allowed him to write about lovely things. Whereas Lorca inherited an aesthetic that allowed him to write about anything— even what he didn't understand. And that was one of the wonderful things that I got from him, and later got from Pablo Neruda—the idea that you could go after these very powerful centers of feeling in you, even if you couldn't parse them.

And these powerful feelings might be political feelings?

Yeah. They might be rage. Lorca's *Poet in New York* is really at its best a book of rage—of confusion. He doesn't understand what the hell New York is; he hates the sense of its commercial enslavement. He's a rural guy faced with the most industrialized and mechanized island in the world, and he's confused and enraged and, of course, bitterly lonely and isolated. And he writes a great book—the best book of poems ever written about New York City. There's one particular poem, the one that I quote in that essay, called "New York: Office and Denunciation," in which you just hear that surging anger. It was a poem I read when I was very young and it just stayed with me, and I kept saying, "This is the avenue, this is the avenue. I've got to stop trying to be so rational about what I can't be rational about."

For me, the politics never come in very directly. They usually enter in through the characters and the story. I would never sacrifice the character—the person who I felt something for—for the politics. If this beautiful guy happens to own Sears, so be it. I'm not going to make him a farmworker just to make a point.

When you speak of rage, and of realizing you can't be rational, it sounds like the poem "They Feed They Lion." In terms of form and voice, that poem seems unique in your whole body of work. Is that fair to say?

Yes, it is. I really don't know how it came into being. But I do remember that I had the idea for it and waited several days before I wrote it. I kept saying to myself, "I'm not ready to write this. I want to wait, and just let it germinate."

What was that initial idea? Can you put it in a nutshell?

The first thing that came into my mind? I had the title, which derived entirely from a statement that was made to me. I was working alongside a guy in Detroit—a black guy named Eugene—when I was probably about twenty-four. He was a somewhat older guy, and we were sorting universal joints, which are part of the drivetrain of a car. The guy who owned the place had bought used ones, and we were supposed to sort the ones that could be rebuilt and made into usable replacement parts from the ones that were too badly damaged. So we spread them out on the concrete floor, and we were looking at them carefully, because we were the guys who'd then do the job of rebuilding them. We had two sacks that we were putting them in—burlap sacks—and at one point Eugene held up a sack, and on it were the words "Detroit Municipal Zoo." And he laughed, and said, "They feed they lion they meal in they sacks." That's exactly what he said! And I thought, This guy's a genius with language. He laughed when he said it, because he knew that he was speaking an English that I didn't speak, but that I would understand, of course. He was almost parodying it, even though he appreciated the loveliness of it. It stuck in my mind, and then one night just after the riots in

Detroit—I'd gone back to the city to see what had happened—somehow I thought of that line. "There's a poem there," I said. "But I don't know what it is. And I'm just going to walk around for a couple of days and see what accumulates."

I waited two days, got a good night's sleep, and got up in the morning and wrote the damn thing. It struck me that it was a long line and that it would be out of the poet Christopher Smart. Do you know his work? He's an eighteenth-century mystical poet, a great poet, and his greatest poem was written in a madhouse. We only have a fragment of it. It's a sort of call-and-response poem—very incantatory. I said, "That's the rhythm I'm going to try to use." It's the only time I've ever tried to utilize that rhythm successfully.

There is a kind of incantatory mode in a lot of your other poems—a repetition of verb phrases, for example—that is very effective.

Yes—as long as I don't get too carried away!

You've written a lot about Spain and your attraction to modern Spanish poets such as Antonio Machado and García Lorca. You've also been drawn to nonliterary figures of the Spanish Civil War, such as the anarchist leaders Buenaventura Durruti and Francisco Ascaso. Why the strong identification with Spain? What drew you to anarchism?

As a young boy I was told that my ancestry was Spanish. Why my parents, both born in a little shtetl in western Russia, would tell me this, I have no idea. But it may have had something to do with the expulsion of the Jews from Spain in 1492. I did notice when I lived in Barcelona that people would just walk up to me and start speaking Catalan, because I looked just like them. And then the Spanish Civil War was the war of my growing up, and many young men from my neighborhood went to it. About half of them came home. So this was my war, in a sense. I was growing up with the mythology of it.

As I got older I began reading the histories of the Spanish Civil War. In the Hugh Thomas history, which is sort of the official biography of the war, I came across the anarchists. They were the ones that impressed me the most, because they were by far the most idealistic, and they had by far, I thought, the most interesting vision of the future. Their willingness to sacrifice in an endless battle for human justice and decency—their willingness to take everything the world could dish out and still keep coming back—seemed boundless. I was just so filled with awe.

For many years I really thought of myself as an anarchist. And then I stopped. But these guys still remain my heroes, because of their gift to humanity and their vision, which was large: we are the stewards of the earth, we don't own anything, and our function is to make it as good as possible and to pass it on to those who are to come. I thought that was a very beautiful vision.

And you saw it as something distinct from the socialism that you undoubtedly were aware of and were exposed to?

Oh, yeah—I saw it as truly revolutionary. Socialism I saw as a kind of peel-and-patch process: peel off some of the uglier aspects and we'll patch it up a little. But anarchism was a radical change: we'll go right to the denominator and destroy it; we'll start all over. We'll abolish the notion of private property; we'll abolish money. Then we'll abolish, of course, all those relationships that are built out of money: marriage, serfdom, racism, colonialism, consumerism, the ills of America.

Did you really think this was something that might happen?

No—I wasn't crazy! I thought it was something I could incorporate in the way I lived—and incorporate in my poetry. But after some years I felt that if even I couldn't incorporate it in myself—and I was given to a love for it—how the hell was it going to grab onto the American earth?

It's like asking somebody who's a practicing Christian whether they can really live by the Sermon on the Mount.

That's exactly right. What was I going to do, take these suburban Republicans and turn them into that little flock around Jesus Christ?

In The Bread of Time *you say that Antonio Machado's poetry is written "with such simplicity and clarity we come to believe him absolutely, and in doing so we come to understand our own deepest experiences and to believe entirely in their authenticity." And then you say, "It is hard to imagine a more useful poetry." What do you mean by a "useful" poetry? Useful in what way?*

Useful in its largest sense—that is to say, validating one's own experience, validating one's own sense of self. Experience is universal—our experiences are what we share with others.

That was something I found in Machado. The simple clarification of mood, of one's response to basic and simple things—loneliness, the rhythm of walking out in the road, nightfall, dawn, the beauty of plants, the sound of water running downhill. He's able to transform all these essentially simple things into a kind of wholeness and holiness. And it seemed to me that Machado was able to validate these very basic experiences that we all share—and that we begin to think of, in our busy lives, as marginal. But Machado brings them into the center of his experience and his poetry. And I thought, Oh what genius that was, to take what we've marginalized and pull it into the center and make it what sheds light on everything else.

In that way it was a very useful poetry. It gave me a vision of the significance of what was around me, and of my own significance—not because I was special, but because I was *not* special, or at least no more special than anybody else. There was a soothing, almost religious dimension to him, without his ever insisting on being in the least religious. And I thought, This is a poetry that raises my spirits, that energizes me, that gives me hope to go on, hope that I can be of value. He's a poet I go back to all the time.

Auden said, in his great elegy for Yeats, "Poetry makes nothing happen." Do you believe that? I think the rest of the poem goes on to refute it, but how do you respond to that line? Poetry obviously makes something *happen, doesn't it?*

Oh, I think Auden knew that. I think he meant that poetry isn't going to have an immediate political impact—you know, you won't make anarchists out of the Republican Ladies Club with poetry—and if you need *that* change, do something else. If you're a writer you'd better write propaganda, you'd better write for television—I don't know what you ought to write, but maybe words don't have that kind of impact. Maybe only power does.

But we know that poetry makes things happen. In the long run, look at the immense influence of a poet like Whitman. He really has influenced the way an enormous number of people feel about themselves and feel about America. It took a long time, but his influence just keeps rolling into us. Anybody who lives with "Song of Myself," I think, will feel about himself or herself rather differently because of the experience. That, to me, is the most profound thing. I remember reading Whitman when I was maybe in my early twenties and coming across this line: "There is that lot of me and all so luscious." And I thought, That's not vanity! That is a kind of recognition of the beauty of the self, or the other self. As he keeps saying in the poem, "What I am, you are." And I said, "Why don't I just try to live that? Why am I being this mewling, broke, dumb factory worker, and feeling sorry for myself, when I could get up in the morning and say, 'Philip, there is that lot of you and all so luscious!'" And I tell you, it's a line that just keeps resonating in my life and in my work.

An Interview with Edward Hirsch

What are the reverberations of the word mercy *in the title of your new book?*

First, the *Mercy* is the name of the ship that brings my mother from Europe to the U.S. when she's a girl. As I say in the poem, mercy is something she can never get enough of. I think that reflects my sense of the world, though I'm not sure why. I have received mercy from those I love and about none from those I mistakenly thought loved me. In my Hart Crane–García Lorca poem in *The Simple Truth* I speak of a merciless God who pushed these hideous images at the speaker, who is clearly me, images of my young son falling from the roof he works on, of my father dead. I'm afraid we live at the mercy of a power, maybe a God, without mercy. And yet we find it, as I have, from others.

The word tenderness *comes up in the first poem, "Smoke." How did a feeling of tenderness come into your poems?*

In that poem I list the names of the guys coming out into the morning air after a night of work, Bernie, Stash, Williams, and I. One of us uses the word *tenderness,* and I know it wasn't me. I know who it was, I remember the moment forty-seven years ago in a bar in downriver Detroit. Bernie Strempek and I were watching this beautiful second-rate jazz singer, and Bernie—divining my state of mind—began to speak of tenderness and how above all else it was what he desired. I'm going to sound like a moron, but I had no idea what he was talking about. My thoughts were small and elsewhere. Bernie was a guy of amazing smarts who seemed almost too gentle and

From *American Poet,* "An Interview with Edward Hirsch" (March 1999).

delicate for this world, the world in which he did not long remain. His mother was and still is one of my heroes. The father had abandoned the family of five, and she supported them by working nights at Ford Rouge; furthermore, she totally supported Bernie's wish to become a poet. She appears in two poems in the new book. Years later I heard Galway Kinnell remark how much he valued a poetry of tenderness, and I thought, Wow, I could use some in mine, which at the time was dominated by rage toward American racism and imperialism. In the book *1933* you can see my first efforts in that direction.

I wonder if you would say something about the final three lines of "Reinventing America," which seem to be a description of the Detroit of your boyhood.

> *It was merely village life,*
> *exactly what our parents left in Europe*
> *brought to America with pure fidelity.*

I'm talking about the racial and ethnic hatreds that seemed asleep until they exploded in violence. I have a hunch this was inspired by Williams's *In the American Grain*. Detroit may have been something Europe never knew—though it must know it now—but it did not submit to the new world in the manner that Williams hoped. We lived with the old poisons still intact. An act or more likely a rumored act sets the place on fire. If you were Phil Levine aged fourteen, 5'2", 125 pounds, it was a nightmare. Detroit was the most anti-Semitic city west of Munich, and all these Jew haters—in my imagination—were coming after me, and in fact a few were. But in spite of that the kid in the poem is learning to accommodate all the madness and to live in the eye of the hurricane and survive. In that way the title is not ironic.

Would it be fair to say there's a sense of orphanhood running through this book?

In an odd way, yes. I don't mean I personally felt I was an orphan. My father died when I was five, but I grew up in a strong family. My mother worked full-time, so I was largely ungoverned, free to roam the streets of Detroit from an early age and research the poems to come, a junior Walt Whitman going among powerful, uneducated people. I have a sense that many Americans, especially those like me with European or foreign parents, feel they have to invent their families just as they have to invent themselves.

American poets have sometimes been criticized for writing about their families. Is there any validity in this critique?

American poets have been criticized for anything you can think of. For being too English, recently for not being English enough. For free verse, for formal verse. For being obscure. For assuming words have meaning. For using their imaginations to invent Americas more interesting than the ones they got. For writing about their love lives, for not writing about their love lives. Each of us has a family or doesn't have a family. Those who do might naturally turn to that experience and try to transform it into poetry. Look what Williams did with the elderly women in his family, starting with Emily Dickinson Wellcome. Would we want not to have those poems? The test is the quality of the work. Period.

The poets Vallejo and Lorca come into your new book. What have they meant to you?

More than I can find words for. In *The Bread of Time* I described how *Poet in New York* directed me toward my first decent poems of rage against Detroit and General Motors, for whom I worked. I soon learned not to imitate Lorca. For one thing it's too easy, for another it always shows. Back in 1994 I reread a lot of Lorca to write that essay, and the day I reread *Poet in New York* I put the book down and couldn't stop talking like Lorca. "Hunger is a boy in a dark room with black shoes that pinch," and so on. I was seeing the world through his glasses. Something like that happened when I first visited the Prado back in 1966. I spent more than an hour with Goya's black paintings, and when I left the museum I entered the Madrid of Goya. Wherever I looked I saw the punished bodies, the torn mouths, the eyes bursting with fear or rage.

Vallejo I came to much later, in my early thirties in the translations of Jim Wright, Thomas Merton, Lillian Lowenfels, Nan Braymer, Charles Guenther, which are still the best translations we have. I later learned Spanish and struggled with the originals, which are very difficult, and then two friends, the scholar José Elgorriaga and the Mexican poet Ernesto Trejo, led me patiently through them, and I got an idea of their majesty. If his collected works were available in great translations he'd be as famous here in the States as Neruda.

No one can write like Vallejo and not sound like a fraud. He's just too much himself and not you. I did swipe one thing from him. In his great poem to Pedro Rojas he gives this railroad worker a little silver spoon with which to eat his lunch on the job. It's just a perfect tiny insight into the man. In my poem to P. L., the soldier who died in Spain, I give P. L. a little knife he wears at all times. Maybe someday someone will find the person who gets the fork.

How much do you think of yourself as a poet of work? I think there's a deeper commitment to saving from oblivion what is thought of as ordinary life.

In my twenties, before I learned how to write poems of work, I thought of myself as the person who would capture this world. There'll always be working people in my poems because I grew up with them, and I am a poet of memory. There was always music in the poetry of Jimmy Merrill and Bill Matthews; music was just part of who they were and in their poems still are. For sure I once thought of myself as the poet who would save the ordinary from oblivion. Now I think poetry will save nothing from oblivion, but I keep writing about the ordinary because for me it's the home of the extraordinary, the only home.

Your early years of working in Detroit seem inexhaustible. Do you ever feel you're overdrawing the account?

Probably not nearly as often as others do, especially those who have no idea how poetry comes to be. I write what's given me to write. I don't sit down with the notion, I will celebrate those who work or even those I worked with. I sit down with a pad of paper and a pen. On good days I'm ready to celebrate, as García Lorca would put it, "the constant baptism of newly created things." I see nothing wrong with poems about work or people who work. If half the most celebrated poets want to pay homage to Wittgenstein, I won't complain. Whatever the drive is, we follow it: if the poem is about killing and devouring a rabbit or seducing a statue or singing in an empty warehouse to make my peace with the demons of filth, so be it. All of this may produce garbage, but we do our best.

I love the poem "The Unknowable." Would you say something about its genesis? It seems as if jazz has had a great influence on you as a poet.

The Sonny Rollins poem. I love his sound. I can hear it right now on "Lover Man" with Brownie and Max Roach; it's such a full and unapologetically sensual blooming. In the late Sixties before his second "retirement," he recorded "East Broadway Rundown." I listened to that over and over, couldn't get enough of his sound. What made him my hero was his ability to remove himself from the music scene just at that point in his career when he was becoming the dominant saxophonist, to stop playing publicly and retire into himself and his instrument. For close to two years he lived like a monk alone in Brooklyn, lifting weights, practicing his music on the Williamsburg Bridge when the weather permitted, just living with both of his instruments. That dedication amazed me; he withdrew from the whole commercial thing into the monastery of his art.

I don't know how much the music has influenced my writing; I know it's inspired me, and the young jazz musicians I went to school with in Detroit, Kenny Burrell, Pepper Adams, Bess Bonier, Tommy Flanagan, Barry Harris, were the first people I knew who were living the creative lives of artists. In age they were kids like me, and I thought if they can do it then I can do it. There were many others who did their best and wound up as footnotes, like my friend Marion in the poem "Flowering Midnight," but they too were part of the enterprise. It's just like poetry: you can give it your all and find out later it wasn't enough.

At times you seem to be mythologizing the world of your parents before you were born. Why is that so important to you?

What I inherited were myths and maybe even a few facts. My father's life seemed and still seems utterly mysterious to me. He came alone to the States from Russia at age eleven. He settled in New York City with two sisters and their families. Not until a few years ago I learned there were three sisters. He enlisted in the English army at age nineteen. He was stationed in Palestine. He deserted. He found a new identity and a passport in Cairo. Or maybe none of this happened. I recall a tall, loving, dark, very handsome man, one who spoke perfect English, Yiddish, Russian, who read Latin poetry and Russian and French fiction, who voted for Hoover and not FDR. A Jew voting for Hoover? He was thirty-five when he died. My mother carried on and supported us; her ambition had been to write poetry and songs. I never heard them. They and my grandfather seemed mythic: people who crossed a continent, an ocean, landed in a strange country, learned "our ways, our language," and lived with gusto and style. They mythologized themselves.

There's a revealing moment in "Salt and Oil" in which you say,

> *This is a moment*
> *in the daily life of the world,*
> *a moment that will pass into*
> *the unwritten biography*
> *of your city or my city*
> *unless it is frozen into the fine print*
> *of our eyes.*

Do you see this recent work as saving that moment and writing that unwritten biography?

I want a record, a visual one will do. I'm saying look, here they come, pay attention. Let your eyes transform what appears ordinary, commonplace, into what it is, a moment in time, an observed fragment of eternity. Millions of us are walking the streets, and at any moment literally dozens of us are seeing. I'm saying if you're awake, if I'm awake, this is what we could see. Any one of us can transform the moment into what it is. Salt and Oil are based on two poets I knew and loved who passed from breath before they did the work they were meant to do. The hero of one, Salt, the name I give Bernie Strempek, was Hart Crane. Oil had two heroes, Homer and Rilke. I can't write like either Rilke or Homer, so I fed at the trough of Hart Crane for this poem. Of course there is a third person in the drama, but I never name or describe him. I invite the reader to mortalize him.

I wonder if you'd say something about the structure of The Mercy.

Originally I saw the book very differently, but my editor, Harry Ford, asked me to write a description of the book even before I began to put it together. I wrote one description and my wife disliked it, so I wrote a second in which I called it a book of journeys, from youth to age, from innocence to experience, from sanity to madness and back again. When I then looked at the poetry I'd assembled I saw about fifty pages of it didn't belong; then I had to put the rest together. I quickly saw three sections and a building toward intimacy, intensity. That final section is mainly family poems and includes actual as well as spiritual brothers and sisters and parents. You and Larry Levis helped me with my previous book, and together you gave me the notion of building the sections to a sort of climax and keeping that high into the next section then gradually coming down to rebuild again to another climax. I tried it again. My friend Peter Everwine gave me the notion of the coda at the end, the little elegy for my mother, who died while I was putting the book together. If this is a successful structure I owe it to you, Eddie, and Larry, and Peter. If it's not I still owe it to you, not that I had to take your advice.

Do you know where you're going next?

Brooklyn in April. Not really. I never do. I'm seventy-one now, so it's hard to imagine a dramatic change. I don't expect to embark on anything like *The Cantos* or *The Dream Songs*. Or even a Brooklyn poem based on *Paterson*. It would be nice to stumble onto one of those great projects so I could stay busy right through my dotage, but I'm not counting on it. Work might keep me from turning into an ash tree or a cabbage or a horse's ass. I'll try to keep my ears open in case there's a tune on the wind I should be hearing. I've never known where I'm going until I've gone and come back, and then it takes me ages to see what the trip was about. I've never truly planned a book ahead of time. I know that works for others, and to paraphrase Frost, it might work for me, but it hasn't yet.

Have I forgotten someone or something?

Cesare Pavese. I first read him thirty years ago in a Penguin translation I found in London. I fell in love with his way of making a poem. Then later *Hard Labor* translated by William

Arrowsmith, and I must have read it fifteen times before I found it could help me. He's in this book, he—and as usual— Williams. And for a change Hart Crane and Antonio Machado. But Pavese is the inspiration or maybe the trickster to whom I owe much of this work or whatever is worthy in the book. He blamed himself enough; he doesn't need my fuck-ups on his shoulders.

The Mercy *is dedicated to your mother. Does she cast a retrospective light over the book?*

I was very lucky to have a mother who encouraged me to become a poet. As a fourteen-year-old I fell in love with horse racing, and she hated that. I think she was so glad I quit the track and went to college when I turned eighteen that I could have studied lion taming, and she would have said, "That's an old and honorable profession." But she loved poetry, fiction, music; that a son of hers would devote himself to this art thrilled her. Only the final poem in the book was written after her death, which was in the spring of last year, just after she turned ninety-four. I did not see her death coming. The last time I spoke with her she sounded very snappy and was looking forward to my new book. I hope the book contains some of her zest for life, some of her belief in the power of beauty, some of her great humor. As a teacher you too must have known many young people who wanted to pursue poetry but were discouraged by their families. I'm one lucky guy to have had Esther Levine for my mother.